CompTIA Security+ SY0-701 Certification

Exclusive Preparation

Achieve **success** in your **CompTIA Security+ SY0-701 Exam** on the **first try** with our **new** and **exclusive preparation book.**

This **New book** is **designed** to **help you test** your **knowledge**, **providing** a **collection** of the **latest questions** with **detailed explanations** and **official references.**

Save both **time** and **money** by **investing in this book**, which **covers all the topics included** in the **CompTIA Security+ SY0-701 exam.**

This **book** includes **two full-length, highly important practice tests, each** with **90 questions**, for a **total** of **180 questions.** It also provides **detailed explanations** for **each question** and **official reference links.**

Dedicate your **effort** to **mastering** these **CompTIA Security+ SY0-701 exam questions**, as they **offer up-to-date information** on the **entire exam syllabus.**

This book is **strategically crafted** to not only assess your **knowledge** and **skills** but also to **boost your confidence for the** official exam.

With a focus on **thorough preparation, passing** the **official CompTIA Security+ SY0-701 Exam** on your **first attempt becomes achievable** through **diligent study of these valuable resources.**

The **CompTIA Security+ SY0-701** exam has a **duration of 90 minutes** and contains a **maximum** of **90 questions.**

To pass, candidates need to **score** at least **750 out of 900 points.**

CompTIA Security+ (SY0-701) Exam Domains:

1. General Security Concepts.
2. Threats, Vulnerabilities and Mitigations.
3. Security Architecture.
4. Security Operations.
5. Security Program Management and Oversight.

Welcome!

PRACTICE TEST I

1) Which threat actor is most likely to be recruited by a foreign government to target critical systems in other nations?

A. Hacktivist

B. Whistleblower

C. Organized crime

D. Unskilled attacker

2) What is used to introduce additional complexity prior to employing a one-way data transformation algorithm?

A. Key stretching

B. Data masking

C. Steganography

D. Salting

3) Which type of social engineering attack took place when an employee clicked a link in an email from a payment website, entered their log-in information to update contact information, but received a "page not found" error message?

A. Brand impersonation

B. Pretexting

C. Typosquatting

D. Phishing

4) Which firewall Access Control List (ACL) rule will restrict outbound DNS traffic from an enterprise's internal network to only allow requests from a single device with the IP address 10.50.10.25?

A. Access list outbound permit 0.0.0.0/0 0.0.0.0/0 port 53

Access list outbound deny 10.50.10.25/32 0.0.0.0/0 port 53

B. Access list outbound permit 0.0.0.0/0 10.50.10.25/32 port 53

Access list outbound deny 0.0.0.0/0 0.0.0.0/0 port 53

C. Access list outbound permit 0.0.0.0/0 0.0.0.0/0 port 53

Access list outbound deny 0.0.0.0/0 10.50.10.25/32 port 53

D. Access list outbound permit 10.50.10.25/32 0.0.0.0/0 port 53

Access list outbound deny 0.0.0.0/0 0.0.0.0/0 port 53

5) A data administrator is setting up authentication for a SaaS application and wants to minimize the number of credentials employees have to manage.

The company wants to use domain credentials for accessing new SaaS applications.

Which method would enable this functionality?

A. SSO

B. LEAP

C. MFA

D. PEAP

6) Which scenario below depicts a potential instance of a business email compromise attack?

A. An employee receives a gift card request in an email that has an executive's name in the display field of the email.

B. Employees who open an email attachment receive messages demanding payment in order to access files.

C. A service desk employee receives an email from the HR director asking for log-in credentials to a cloud administrator account.

D. An employee receives an email with a link to a phishing site that is designed to look like the company's email portal.

7) Given that direct access from the database administrators' workstations to the network segment housing the database servers has been blocked, what method should a database administrator employ to reach the database servers?

A. Jump server

B. RADIUS

C. HSM

D. Load balancer

8) To enhance protection against future attacks similar to the one where an organization's internet-facing website was compromised due to a buffer overflow exploit, what measures

should the organization implement?

A. NGFW

B. WAF

C. TLS

D. SD-WAN

9) To prevent similar attacks from succeeding in the future, what steps should the administrator take after noticing several users logging in from suspicious IP addresses, determining that the employees were not logging in from those IPs, and resetting the affected users' passwords?

A. Multifactor authentication

B. Permissions assignment

C. Access management

D. Password complexity

10) Which social engineering techniques are being attempted when an employee receives a text message that appears to be from the payroll department and requests credential verification? (Select two.)

A. Typosquatting

B. Phishing

C. Impersonation

D. Vishing

E. Smishing

F. Misinformation

11) Multiple employees received a deceptive text message purportedly from the Chief Executive Officer (CEO). The message stated:

"I'm in an airport right now with no access to email. I need you to buy gift cards for employee recognition awards. Please send the gift cards to following email address."

What are the most suitable actions to take in this scenario? (Select two.)

A. Cancel current employee recognition gift cards.

B. Add a smishing exercise to the annual company training.

C. Issue a general email warning to the company.

D. Have the CEO change phone numbers.

E. Conduct a forensic investigation on the CEO's phone.

F. Implement mobile device management.

12) A company must use certified hardware for constructing its networks. Which approach most effectively mitigates the risks linked to obtaining counterfeit hardware?

A. A thorough analysis of the supply chain.

B. A legally enforceable corporate acquisition policy.

C. A right to audit clause in vendor contracts and SOWs.

D. An in-depth penetration test of all suppliers and vendors.

13) Which of the following contains information regarding

the terms of engagement with a third-party penetration tester?

A. Rules of engagement

B. Supply chain analysis

C. Right to audit clause

D. Due diligence

14) A penetration tester initiates an engagement by conducting port and service scans on the client's environment, following the rules of engagement. Which of the following reconnaissance types is the tester performing?

A. Active

B. Passive

C. Defensive

D. Offensive

15) What is necessary for an organization to effectively oversee its restoration process in case of system failure?

A. IRP

B. DRP

C. RPO

D. SDLC

16) Which vulnerability is linked to the installation

of software from sources other than the manufacturer's approved software repository?

A. Jailbreaking

B. Memory injection

C. Resource reuse

D. Side loading

17) A security analyst is examining the logs below:

```
[10:00:00 AM] Login rejected - username administrator - password Spring2023
[10:00:01 AM] Login rejected - username jsmith - password Spring2023
[10:00:01 AM] Login rejected - username quest - password Spring2023
[10:00:02 AM] Login rejected - username cpolk - password Spring2023
[10:00:03 AM] Login rejected - username fmartin - password Spring2023
```

What type of attack is most likely taking place?

A. Password spraying

B. Account forgery

C. Pass-the-hash

D. Brute-force

18) An analyst is assessing the implementation of Zero Trust principles in the data plane. Which of the following would be most relevant for the analyst to evaluate?

A. Secured zones

B. Subject role

C. Adaptive identity

D. Threat scope reduction

19) An engineer is seeking a solution to enhance security by preventing unauthorized access to internal company resources. Which of the following would be the best solution?

A. RDP server

B. Jump server

C. Proxy server

D. Hypervisor

20) The company's web filter is set up to examine the URL for specific strings and block access if matches are detected. Which of the following search strings should an analyst employ to prohibit access to non-encrypted websites?

A. encryption=off

B. http://

C. www.*.com

D. :443

21) In response to a security incident, the security operations team noticed continuous network traffic from a malicious IP address, 10.1.4.9. A security analyst is now establishing an inbound firewall rule to prevent the IP address from accessing the organization's network. Which of the following fulfills this request?

A. access-list inbound deny ip source 0.0.0.0/0 destination 10.1.4.9/32

B. access-list inbound deny ip source 10.1.4.9/32 destination 0.0.0.0/0

C. access-list inbound permit ip source 10.1.4.9/32 destination 0.0.0.0/0

D. access-list inbound permit ip source 0.0.0.0/0 destination 10.1.4.9/32

22) A company must grant administrative access to internal resources while restricting the traffic permitted through the security boundary to a minimum. Which of the following methods is most secure?

A. Implementing a bastion host

B. Deploying a perimeter network

C. Installing a WAF

D. Utilizing single sign-on

23) A security analyst is examining SIEM alerts regarding suspicious network traffic originating from an employee's corporate laptop. To proceed with the investigation, the analyst requires further information about the executable running on the machine. Which of the following logs should the analyst use as a data source?

A. Application

B. IPS/IDS

C. Network

D. Endpoint

24) A cybersecurity operations team notifies a security analyst of a new method that malicious actors are employing to infiltrate networks. SIEM alerts have not yet been configured. Which of the following best describes what the security analyst should do to identify this behavior?

A. Digital forensics

B. E-discovery

C. Incident response

D. Threat hunting

25) A company bought cyber insurance to mitigate risks listed on the risk register. Which of the following strategies does this represent?

A. Accept

B. Transfer

C. Mitigate

D. Avoid

26) A security administrator wants to secure data on laptops used by employees. Which encryption technique should the security administrator utilize from the options provided?

A. Partition

B. Asymmetric

C. Full disk

D. Database

27) Which security control type is best represented by an acceptable use policy?

A. Detective

B. Compensating

C. Corrective

D. Preventive

28) The IT manager notifies all help desk staff that only the IT manager and the help desk lead will have access to the administrator console of the help desk software. Which of the following security techniques is the IT manager setting up?

A. Hardening

B. Employee monitoring

C. Configuration enforcement

D. Least privilege

29) Which of the following is the most likely to be utilized for documenting risks, responsible parties, and thresholds?

A. Risk tolerance

B. Risk transfer

C. Risk register

D. Risk analysis

30) What should a security administrator follow when configuring a new set of firewall rules?

A. Disaster recovery plan

B. Incident response procedure

C. Business continuity plan

D. Change management procedure

31) A company is expanding its threat surface program by permitting individuals to perform security testing on the company's internet-facing application. The company will reward researchers according to the vulnerabilities they find. Which of the following best describes the program the company is setting up?

A. Open-source intelligence

B. Bug bounty

C. Red team

D. Penetration testing

32) Which of the following threat actors is most likely to employ significant financial resources to target critical systems in foreign countries?

A. Insider

B. Unskilled attacker

C. Nation-state

D. Hacktivist

33) Which of the following allows the execution of commands, which can view or manipulate data, through an input field?

A. Cross-site scripting

B. Side loading

C. Buffer overflow

D. SQL injection

34) Employees in the research and development business unit undergo comprehensive training to ensure they are well-versed in safeguarding company data. Which of the following is the type of data these employees are most likely to use in day-to-day work activities?

A. Encrypted

B. Intellectual property

C. Critical

D. Data in transit

35) A company has started affixing asset inventory stickers to all laptops and linking them to employee IDs. Which of the following security benefits do these actions provide? (Choose two.)

A. If a security incident occurs on the device, the correct employee can be notified.

B. The security team will be able to send user awareness training to the appropriate device.

C. Users can be mapped to their devices when configuring software MFA tokens.

D. User-based firewall policies can be correctly targeted to the appropriate laptops.

E. When conducting penetration testing, the security team will be able to target the desired laptops.

F. Company data can be accounted for when the employee leaves the organization.

36) A technician aims to enhance the situational and environmental awareness of current users as they switch from remote work to office work. Which of the following is the best option?

A. Send out periodic security reminders.

B. Update the content of new hire documentation.

C. Modify the content of recurring training.

D. Implement a phishing campaign.

37) A newly appointed board member with cybersecurity expertise is requesting a quarterly report for the board of directors that outlines the number of incidents affecting the organization. The systems administrator is creating a method to present the data to the board of directors. Which of the following should the systems administrator use?

A. Packet captures

B. Vulnerability scans

C. Metadata

D. Dashboard

38) A systems administrator gets the following alert from a file integrity monitoring tool:

The hash of the cmd.exe file has changed.

The systems administrator reviews the operating system logs and observes that no patches have been applied in the past two months. Which of the following most likely occurred?

A. The end user changed the file permissions.

B. A cryptographic collision was detected.

C. A snapshot of the file system was taken.

D. A rootkit was deployed.

39) In the shared responsibility model, which role is responsible for securing the company's database in an Infrastructure as a Service (IaaS) model for a cloud environment?

A. Client

B. Third-party vendor

C. Cloud provider

D. DBA

40) A client requested that a security company supply a document detailing the project, its cost, and the expected

completion time frame. Which of the following documents should the company provide to the client?

A. MSA

B. SLA

C. BPA

D. SOW

41) To enhance the strength of a password and deter hackers from cracking it, a random string of 36 characters was appended to the password. Which of the following best describes this technique?

A. Key stretching

B. Tokenization

C. Data masking

D. Salting

42) A company wishes to verify the origin of the software it is deploying to ensure it originated from the vendor from which the software was purchased. Which of the following is the best way for the company to confirm this information?

A. Validate the code signature.

B. Execute the code in a sandbox.

C. Search the executable for ASCII strings.

D. Generate a hash of the files.

43) A security analyst is examining an application server and finds that the software on the server is exhibiting unusual behavior. The software typically executes batch jobs locally without generating any traffic. However, the process is currently producing outbound traffic on random high ports. Which of the following vulnerabilities has likely been exploited in this software?

A. Memory injection

B. Race condition

C. Side loading

D. SQL injection

44) What would be the most useful approach to determine if the long-term cost of transferring a risk is lower than the impact of the risk?

A. ARO

B. RTO

C. RPO

D. ALE

E. SLE

45) A security analyst is alerted to an internal system sending an unusually high volume of DNS queries to internet systems over brief periods, occurring outside of business hours. Which of the following is most likely occurring?

A. A worm is propagating across the network.

B. Data is being exfiltrated.

C. A logic bomb is deleting data.

D. Ransomware is encrypting files.

46) A company is strategizing a disaster recovery site to guarantee that a solitary natural disaster would not lead to the total loss of regulated backup data. Which of the following should the company consider?

A. Geographic dispersion

B. Platform diversity

C. Hot site

D. Load balancing

47) What should a systems administrator utilize to facilitate the smooth deployment of resources within the cloud provider?

A. Software as a service

B. Infrastructure as code

C. Internet of Things

D. Software-defined networking

48) Following a recent vulnerability scan, a security engineer must strengthen the routers in the corporate network. Which of the following is the most appropriate to disable?

A. Console access

B. Routing protocols

C. VLANs

D. Web-based administration

49) A security analyst discovers a potentially malicious video file on a server and requires identifying both the file's creation date and its creator. Which of the following actions would most likely give the security analyst the information required?

A. Obtain the file's SHA-256 hash.

B. Use hexdump on the file's contents.

C. Check endpoint logs.

D. Query the file's metadata.

50) An analyst received a security bulletin from one of the company's vendors advising a BIOS update. Which of the following vulnerability types is being addressed by the patch?

A. Virtualization

B. Firmware

C. Application

D. Operating system

51) A systems administrator aims to restrict user access to data according to their roles and responsibilities. The administrator also seeks to implement the necessary access structure through a simplified format. Which of the following

should the administrator apply to the site recovery resource group?

A. RBAC

B. ACL

C. SAML

D. GPO

52) End users at a company are reporting an inability to access external websites. Upon reviewing the performance data of the DNS servers, the analyst finds that the CPU, disk, and memory usage are low, while the network interface is overwhelmed with inbound traffic. Network logs show only a small number of DNS queries sent to this server. Which of the following best describes what the security analyst is seeing?

A. Concurrent session usage

B. Secure DNS cryptographic downgrade

C. On-path resource consumption

D. Reflected denial of service

53) An organization is facing scalability challenges with its VPN concentrator and internet circuit as a result of remote work. The organization seeks a software solution to minimize traffic on the VPN and internet circuit, while ensuring encrypted tunnel access to the data center and monitoring of remote employee internet traffic. Which of the following will help achieve these objectives?

A. Deploying a SASE solution to remote employees.

B. Building a load-balanced VPN solution with redundant internet.

C. Purchasing a low-cost SD-WAN solution for VPN traffic.

D. Using a cloud provider to create additional VPN concentrators.

54) The local administrator account of a company's VPN appliance was used unexpectedly to log into the remote management interface. Which of the following would have most likely prevented this from happening'?

A. Using least privilege

B. Changing the default password

C. Assigning individual user IDs

D. Reviewing logs more frequently

55) A company is collaborating with a vendor to conduct a penetration test. Which of the following includes an estimate about the number of hours required to complete the engagement?

A. SOW

B. BPA

C. SLA

D. NDA

56) Which of the following teams integrates offensive and defensive testing methods to safeguard an organization's critical systems?

A. Red

B. Blue

C. Purple

D. Yellow

57) Which risk management strategy should an enterprise prioritize initially if a legacy application is crucial to business operations and some preventive controls remain unimplemented?

A. Mitigate

B. Accept

C. Transfer

D. Avoid

58) Which incident response activity ensures that evidence is handled properly?

A. E-discovery

B. Chain of custody

C. Legal hold

D. Preservation

59) Which of the following defines the highest level of risk that an organization is willing to accept?

A. Risk indicator

B. Risk level

C. Risk score

D. Risk threshold

60) A company needs to ensure that sensitive data at rest is encrypted to make it unreadable. Which of the following will the company most likely use?

A. Hashing

B. Tokenization

C. Encryption

D. Segmentation

61) Visitors to a secure facility must check in with a photo ID and gain entry through an access control vestibule. Which of the following but describes this form of security control?

A. Physical

B. Managerial

C. Technical

D. Operational

62) A company is preparing to establish a SIEM system and designate an analyst to conduct weekly reviews of the logs. Which of the following types of controls is the company setting up?

A. Corrective

B. Preventive

C. Detective

D. Deterrent

63) A systems administrator is updating the password policy across an enterprise environment and aims to implement this change on all systems as expeditiously as possible. Which of the following operating system security measures will the administrator most likely use?

A. Deploying PowerShell scripts

B. Pushing GPO update

C. Enabling PAP

D. Updating EDR profiles

64) What action can be taken to ensure that a security analyst can accurately assess the overall risk to an organization when a new vulnerability is disclosed?

A. A full inventory of all hardware and software.

B. Documentation of system classifications.

C. A list of system owners and their departments.

D. Third-party risk assessment documentation.

65) An employee receives a text message from an unfamiliar number, purportedly from the company's Chief Executive Officer, requesting the purchase of several gift cards. Which of the following types of attacks does this describe?

A. Vishing

B. Smishing

C. Pretexting

D. Phishing

66) A system was compromised by a hacker who gained access through a phishing attempt, which occurred when a user clicked on a suspicious link. The link, once clicked, spread ransomware laterally across the network, where it remained inactive for several weeks. Which of the following would have mitigated the spread?

A. IPS

B. IDS

C. WAF

D. UAT

67) A security engineer is deploying Full Disk Encryption (FDE) on all laptops within an organization. Which of the following are the most important for the engineer to consider as part of the planning process? (Select two).

A. Key escrow

B. TPM presence

C. Digital signatures

D. Data tokenization

E. Public key management

F. Certificate authority linking

68) An administrator is examining the security logs of a single server and finds the following:

```
Keywords  Date and Time   Source              Event ID Task Category
--------  --------------  ------------------  -------- -------------
Audit     09/16/2022      Microsoft           4625     Logon
Failure   11:13:05 AM     Windows security
Audit     09/16/2022      Microsoft           4625     Logon
Failure   11:13:07 AM     Windows security
Audit     09/16/2022      Microsoft           4625     Logon
Failure   11:13:09 AM     Windows security
Audit     09/16/2022      Microsoft           4625     Logon
Failure   11:13:11 AM     Windows security
Audit     09/16/2022      Microsoft           4625     Logon
Failure   11:13:13 AM     Windows security
Audit     09/16/2022      Microsoft           4625     Logon
Failure   11:13:15 AM     Windows security
Audit     09/16/2022      Microsoft           4625     Logon
Failure   11:13:17 AM     Windows security
Audit     09/16/2022      Microsoft           4625     Logon
Failure   11:13:19 AM     Windows security
Audit     09/16/2022      Microsoft           4625     Logon
Failure   11:13:21 AM     Windows security
Audit     09/16/2022      Microsoft           4625     Logon
Failure   11:13:23 AM     Windows security
Audit     09/16/2022      Microsoft           4625     Logon
Failure   11:13:25 AM     Windows security
Audit     09/16/2022      Microsoft           4625     Logon
Failure   11:13:27 AM     Windows security
```

Which of the following best characterizes the activity recorded in this log file?

A. Brute-force attack

B. Privilege escalation

C. Failed password audit

D. Forgotten password by the user

69) As part of the onboarding process, an employee is required to generate a password for an intranet account. The password must consist of ten characters, including numbers and letters, as well as two special characters. After creating the password, the company will provide the employee with access to other company-owned websites based on their intranet profile. Which of the following access management principles is the company likely employing to protect intranet accounts and authorize access to multiple sites based on a user's intranet account? (Choose two).

A. Federation

B. Identity proofing

C. Password complexity

D. Default password changes

E. Password manager

F. Open authentication

70) An enterprise has faced targeted attacks aimed at exploiting vulnerabilities in outdated browser versions using widely known exploits. Which security solution is best suited to be configured for monitoring and blocking these known signature-based attacks?

A. ACL

B. DLP

C. IDS

D. IPS

71) A company has opted to transition its operations to the cloud. It seeks technology that will prohibit users from downloading company applications for personal purposes, limit the data that can be uploaded, and provide insight into the applications being utilized across the organization. Which of the following solutions will best meet these requirements?

A. An NGFW

B. A CASB

C. Application whitelisting

D. An NG-SWG

72) A systems administrator employed at a local hospital is tasked with guaranteeing the protection and security of patient data. Which of the following data classifications should be used to secure patient data?

A. Public

B. Sensitive

C. Critical

D. Private

73) A systems administrator configured a perimeter firewall but is still observing dubious connections between internal endpoints. Which of the following should be set up in order to mitigate the threat posed by the suspicious activity?

A. Host-based firewall

B. Web application firewall

C. Access control list

D. Application allow list

74) A small business utilizes kiosks on the sales floor to exhibit product information for customers. The security team uncovers that the kiosks are running on end-of-life operating systems. Which of the following is the security team most likely to document as a security implication of the current architecture?

A. Patch availability

B. Product software compatibility

C. Ease of recovery

D. Cost of replacement

75) A company mandates that hard drives be securely wiped prior to sending decommissioned systems for recycling. Which of the following best describes this policy?

A. Enumeration

B. Sanitization

C. Destruction

D. Inventory

76) **An organization is constructing a new backup data center with cost-effectiveness as the primary requirement and Recovery Time Objective (RTO) and Recovery Point Objective (RPO) values set at approximately two days. Which of the following types of sites is the best for this scenario?**

A. Real-time recovery

B. Hot

C. Cold

D. Warm

77) **Following a recent ransomware attack on the company's system, an administrator examined the log files. Which of the following control types did the administrator use?**

A. Compensating

B. Detective

C. Preventive

D. Corrective

78) **A technician is configuring firewall ports to allow traffic for a new system being deployed and supported by a SaaS provider. Which of the following is a risk in the new system?**

A. Default credentials

B. Non-segmented network

C. Supply chain vendor

D. Vulnerable software

79) While troubleshooting a firewall configuration, a technician decides to add a "deny any" policy at the end of the Access Control List (ACL). After implementing the new policy, several company servers become unreachable. Which of the following actions would prevent this issue?

A. Documenting the new policy in a change request and submitting the request to change management.

B. Testing the policy in a non-production environment before enabling the policy in the production network.

C. Disabling any intrusion prevention signatures on the 'deny any' policy prior to enabling the new policy.

D. Including an 'allow any1 policy above the 'deny any' policy.

80) Which of the following best practices provides administrators with a defined timeframe to make changes to an operational system, ensuring availability and minimizing business impacts?

A. Impact analysis

B. Scheduled downtime

C. Backout plan

D. Change management boards

81) An organization seeks a third-party vendor to conduct a penetration test focusing on a specific device. The organization has supplied fundamental details regarding the device. Which of the following best describes this kind of penetration test?

A. Partially known environment

B. Unknown environment

C. Integrated

D. Known environment

82) A Chief Information Security Officer (CISO) intends to specifically highlight the rise of ransomware-as-a-service in a report to the management team. Which of the following best describes the threat actor in the CISO's report?

A. Insider threat

B. Hacktivist

C. Nation-state

D. Organized crime

83) A security architect at a large, multinational organization is worried about the challenges and administrative burden associated with securely managing numerous encryption keys in a multicloud provider environment. The security architect seeks a solution that offers minimal latency to integrate the organization's current keys and to ensure uniform, centralized control and management regardless of the data's location. Which of the following would best meet the architect's

objectives?

A. Trusted Platform Module

B. IaaS

C. HSMaaS

D. PaaS

84) A systems administrator is developing a script to streamline account creation for a large number of end users, aiming to save time and reduce the risk of human error. Which of the following would be a good use case for this task?

A. Off-the-shelf software

B. Orchestration

C. Baseline

D. Policy enforcement

85) Which of the following enables the assignment of messages to specific individuals?

A. Adaptive identity

B. Non-repudiation

C. Authentication

D. Access logs

86) Which of the following factors are crucial to consider when developing a training curriculum for a security

awareness program? (Choose two).

A. Channels by which the organization communicates with customers.

B. The reporting mechanisms for ethics violations.

C. Threat vectors based on the industry in which the organization operates.

D. Secure software development training for all personnel.

E. Cadence and duration of training events.

F. Retraining requirements for individuals who fail phishing simulations.

87) A security administrator requires a method to protect data in an environment that includes mechanisms to monitor and trace any modifications. Which of the following should the administrator set up to achieve this goal?

A. SPF

B. GPO

C. NAC

D. FIM

88) A security consultant requires secure, remote access to a client's environment. What is the most likely tool or method the security consultant should use to obtain access?

A. EAP

B. DHCP

C. IPSec

D. NAT

89) An organization deactivated unnecessary services and installed a firewall in front of a legacy system critical to its operations. Which of the following best describes the actions taken by the organization?

A. Exception

B. Segmentation

C. Risk transfer

D. Compensating controls

90) A company is amending its Acceptable Use Policy (AUP) to prohibit employees from altering the operating system on mobile devices. Which of the following vulnerabilities is the organization addressing?

A. Cross-site scripting

B. Buffer overflow

C. Jailbreaking

D. Side loading

ANSWERS AND EXPLANATION

1) Of the choices provided, the threat actor most likely to be recruited by a foreign government is:

C. Organized crime

Here's why:

Hacktivists are typically motivated by ideology or social change, not financial gain. While some might be swayed by a foreign government's agenda, it's less likely.

Whistleblowers expose wrongdoing, not target critical systems. They might be a target for foreign governments, but not for recruitment.

Unskilled attackers lack the expertise needed for such a task.

Organized crime groups possess the technical skills, resources, and potential for financial gain that a foreign government might offer in exchange for targeting critical systems.

2) D. Salting

Salting involves adding random data to the input of a one-way hash function to ensure that the same input will produce different hash values, thus making it more difficult for attackers to use precomputed hash tables (rainbow tables) to reverse engineer the original input.

3) D. Phishing

Here's why:

Brand impersonation is a broader term encompassing any situation where someone pretends to be a legitimate brand. Phishing is a specific type of brand impersonation that uses emails or websites to steal user credentials.

Pretexting involves creating a fake scenario or story to trick someone into revealing information. There's no mention of a fake story in this case.

Typosquatting involves registering domain names with misspelled versions of legitimate websites to trick users into entering their information on a fake site. There's no indication a misspelled domain was used here.

Phishing perfectly fits the scenario. The email impersonated a payment website (brand impersonation) and tricked the employee into clicking a link (likely to a fake website) and entering their login information (stealing credentials). Even though they received an error message, the attacker might still have captured some information during the process.

The scenario described corresponds to option D, Phishing. Phishing involves sending deceptive emails or messages that appear to be from a legitimate source to trick individuals into providing sensitive information such as usernames, passwords, or financial information. In this case, the employee clicked on a link in an email that purported to be from a payment website.

4) The correct ACL rule to restrict outbound DNS traffic is:

D. Access list outbound permit 10.50.10.25/32 0.0.0.0/0 port 53

Access list outbound deny 0.0.0.0/0 0.0.0.0/0 port 53

Here's why this rule works:

First rule (permit): This rule allows outbound traffic on port 53 (DNS) specifically from the device with IP address 10.50.10.25/32. The destination is set to 0.0.0.0/0, which represents any IP address, allowing the device to reach any DNS server on the internet.

Second rule (deny): This rule denies all other outbound traffic on port 53. Since the permit rule is placed before the deny rule (ACLs are processed sequentially), any outbound DNS request that doesn't originate from 10.50.10.25 will be blocked by this rule.

This configuration allows outbound DNS requests from the specific IP address 10.50.10.25 and denies outbound DNS requests from any other IP address.

Explanation of incorrect options:

A and C: These options allow all outbound DNS traffic (port 53) regardless of the source IP address. They don't achieve the desired restriction.

B: This option permits outbound DNS traffic only to the device 10.50.10.25, which wouldn't allow the device to resolve external DNS names.

5) The method that would enable the data administrator to

achieve this functionality is:

A. SSO (Single Sign-On)

Here's why SSO is the best fit:

SSO (Single Sign-On): This method allows users to access multiple applications with a single login using their existing domain credentials. This eliminates the need for separate credentials for each SaaS application.

LEAP (Lightweight Extensible Authentication Protocol): LEAP is an older EAP type used for wireless network authentication. It doesn't address managing credentials across multiple applications.

MFA (Multi-Factor Authentication): MFA adds an extra layer of security to the authentication process but doesn't directly solve the issue of managing multiple credentials.

PEAP (Protected Extensible Authentication Protocol): Similar to LEAP, PEAP is another EAP type for network authentication and doesn't address managing application credentials.

By implementing SSO, the data administrator can leverage the existing domain credentials for accessing new SaaS applications, reducing credential fatigue for employees.

Single Sign-On (SSO) enables users to authenticate once with their domain credentials and then access multiple applications without needing to re-enter their credentials each time. This aligns with the company's preference to use domain credentials and reduces the burden of managing multiple sets of credentials for different applications.

6) The scenario that depicts a potential business email compromise attack is:

C. A service desk employee receives an email from the HR director asking for log-in credentials to a cloud administrator account.

Here's why:

Business Email Compromise (BEC) attacks specifically target employees to trick them into revealing sensitive information or taking actions that benefit the attacker.

In this scenario, the attacker is impersonating the HR director (display name spoofing) to target a service desk employee who might have access to privileged accounts like a cloud administrator.

If successful, the attacker could gain access to the cloud administrator account and potentially steal data or manipulate configurations.

In a BEC attack, the attacker typically impersonates a high-ranking executive or authority figure within the organization and requests sensitive information or actions from employees. In this case, the HR director is requesting log-in credentials for a cloud administrator account, which is a classic example of BEC where the attacker seeks to gain access to privileged accounts through deception.

The other options are not the best fit for BEC:

A (gift card request) and D (phishing to email portal) are more typical phishing attempts aiming to steal user credentials directly.

B (ransomware) involves malware that encrypts files and demands payment for decryption. While BEC attacks can be used to deploy malware, the scenario itself doesn't directly indicate this.

7) The most suitable method for a database administrator to reach the database servers when direct access is blocked is:

A. Jump server

Here's why:

Jump server: This is a secure server specifically configured to allow authorized users access to other servers on the network. It acts as an intermediary, adding an extra layer of security and control. Database administrators could log in to the jump server and then securely connect to the database servers through a controlled and monitored session.

RADIUS (Remote Authentication Dial-In User Service): While RADIUS is used for authentication, it doesn't directly provide access to servers. It's more focused on network access control.

HSM (Hardware Security Module): HSMs are secure devices used for storing and managing cryptographic keys. They wouldn't be the primary method for accessing database servers.

Load balancer: Load balancers distribute incoming traffic across multiple servers. They aren't designed for individual user access to specific servers like database servers.

Using a jump server provides a secure and auditable way for database administrators to access the servers while maintaining network segmentation and access control.

8) The most effective measure to address a buffer overflow exploit on an internet-facing website is:

B. WAF (Web Application Firewall)

Here's why:

Buffer overflow exploits typically target vulnerabilities in web applications. A WAF specifically inspects incoming traffic directed at web applications and can detect and block malicious attempts to exploit these vulnerabilities, including buffer overflows.

NGFW (Next-Generation Firewall): While NGFWs offer broader security features, they might not be specifically designed to detect application-layer attacks like buffer overflows.

TLS (Transport Layer Security): While TLS encrypts communication between the web server and the client, it doesn't directly prevent buffer overflow vulnerabilities within the web application itself.

SD-WAN (Software-Defined Wide Area Network): SD-WAN is a technology for managing and optimizing traffic across geographically dispersed networks. It doesn't directly address application security vulnerabilities.

By implementing a WAF, the organization can add a layer of protection specifically designed to detect and block web application vulnerabilities like buffer overflows, improving the security of their internet-facing website.

9) The most crucial step the administrator should take to prevent similar attacks in the future is:

A. Multifactor authentication (MFA)

Here's why:

Multifactor authentication (MFA) adds an extra layer of security beyond just passwords. Even if an attacker obtains a user's password through techniques like phishing, they wouldn't be able to log in without the additional factor, such as a verification code sent to the user's phone or a fingerprint scan.

This significantly reduces the risk of successful logins from unauthorized sources.

Permissions assignment and Access management are important security practices, but they wouldn't necessarily prevent unauthorized login attempts in this scenario.

Password complexity can help to a certain extent, but it's not enough on its own. Even complex passwords can be stolen through phishing or brute-force attacks. MFA provides a stronger second layer of defense.

By implementing MFA, the administrator significantly strengthens login security and makes it much harder for attackers to gain access to user accounts, even if they compromise passwords.

10) Two social engineering techniques are being attempted in this scenario:

C. Impersonation: This is a broader social engineering technique where someone pretends to be a trusted person or organization. In this case, the attacker pretends to be from the payroll department.

E. Smishing: This is a specific type of phishing attack that uses SMS text messages to trick victims into revealing personal information or clicking on malicious links. Here, the attacker impersonates the payroll department through a text message.

Here's why the other options are not the best fit:

A. Typosquatting: This involves registering domain names with misspelled versions of legitimate websites. It wouldn't apply to text messages.

B. Phishing (already included in E. Smishing): Phishing is the overall category of deception for stealing information, and smishing is a specific type of phishing using SMS.

D. Vishing: This is similar to phishing but uses voice calls instead of text messages.

F. Misinformation: Misinformation refers to spreading false or inaccurate information. While it could be a social engineering tactic, it's not the primary technique here. The attacker is actively trying to deceive the employee for credential theft.

11) The two most suitable actions to take in this scenario are:

B. Add a smishing exercise to the annual company training. This will help employees recognize the tactics used in smishing attacks and how to respond appropriately. Training can include examples of smishing attempts, red flags to watch out for, and what to do if they suspect a smishing message.

C. Issue a general email warning to the company. This will quickly alert employees about the smishing attempt and advise them to be cautious of any unsolicited requests for gift cards or financial transactions, especially via text messages, even if they appear to come from high-level executives.

Here's why the other options are not the best choices:

A. Cancel current employee recognition gift cards: This might not be necessary unless there's evidence the attackers already gained access to some information. It's better to be cautious but avoid disrupting legitimate processes.

D. Have the CEO change phone numbers: While possible, it's an inconvenience and doesn't guarantee future attempts won't be made by spoofing the CEO's number or impersonating other executives.

E. Conduct a forensic investigation on the CEO's phone: This is an extreme step unless there's a strong suspicion the CEO's phone itself is compromised. It's more likely the attacker is spoofing the CEO's number.

F. Implement mobile device management (MDM): While MDM can be a good security practice overall, it might not directly address employees being deceived by social engineering tactics like smishing. Training and awareness are crucial in this case.

12) The most effective approach to mitigate the risks of obtaining counterfeit hardware is:

A. A thorough analysis of the supply chain.

Here's why:

Supply chain analysis allows you to proactively assess the entire process of acquiring hardware, from the manufacturer to the final delivery. This includes examining distributors, resellers, and any other entities involved. By identifying potential vulnerabilities in the chain, you can avoid counterfeit hardware from entering your network in the first place.

A legally enforceable corporate acquisition policy (B): While having a policy that emphasizes ethical sourcing is important, it can't guarantee the authenticity of hardware. Malicious actors might find ways to circumvent such policies.

A right to audit clause in vendor contracts and SOWs (C): While audit clauses provide some oversight, they might not be enough to uncover sophisticated counterfeiting operations. Audits typically happen after a purchase, and some counterfeiters might be able to bypass detection during a one-time audit.

An in-depth penetration test of all suppliers and vendors (D): Penetration testing focuses on exploiting vulnerabilities in systems, not necessarily identifying counterfeit hardware. While it's a valuable security practice, it's not the most effective method for this specific scenario.

By conducting a thorough analysis of the supply chain, you can gain a deeper understanding of your vendors' practices, identify potential risks, and implement measures to mitigate them. This could involve partnering with reputable distributors, requiring certificates of authenticity from manufacturers, or implementing physical inspection procedures for received hardware.

13) The document containing information regarding the terms of engagement with a third-party penetration tester is:

A. Rules of Engagement (ROE)

Here's why:

Rules of Engagement (ROE) is a formal document that outlines the expectations and limitations of a penetration testing engagement. It details what systems are in scope, what methodologies can be used by the testers, communication procedures, and reporting guidelines. Essentially, it defines the "rules of the game" for both the company and the penetration testing team.

Supply chain analysis (B): This focuses on assessing the security of the entire process of acquiring goods and services, not the specific terms with a penetration tester.

Right to audit clause (C): This clause might be included in a contract with a vendor, but it wouldn't necessarily detail the terms of engagement for a penetration test.

Due diligence (D): Due diligence is a broader term encompassing the investigation of a potential business partner or investment. While it might involve reviewing the penetration tester's capabilities, the ROE would be the specific document outlining the engagement details.

14) The penetration tester is performing A. Active reconnaissance.

Here's why:

Active reconnaissance involves directly interacting with the target system to gather information. In this case, the tester is actively scanning ports and services on the client's network, which solicits responses from the systems themselves. This reveals details about the systems and potential vulnerabilities.

Passive reconnaissance involves gathering information about the target system without directly interacting with it. This might involve looking for information from publicly available sources like social media, DNS records, or network traffic leaks.

Defensive reconnaissance isn't a typical term used in penetration testing. Penetration testing is an offensive activity that aims to identify vulnerabilities.

Offensive reconnaissance is another term for active reconnaissance used in the context of penetration testing.

15) The most necessary element for an organization to effectively oversee its restoration process in case of system failure is:

B. DRP (Disaster Recovery Plan)

Here's why:

DRP (Disaster Recovery Plan): This plan outlines the procedures and steps to be taken for recovering critical IT infrastructure and data in the event of a system failure or disaster. It includes details on restoring systems, recovering data, resuming operations, and minimizing downtime. An effective DRP ensures a well-coordinated and efficient restoration process.

IRP (Incident Response Plan) (A): While IRPs are crucial for responding to security incidents, they focus on containing and eradicating the incident itself, not necessarily the entire restoration process. DRPs encompass a broader scope that includes recovery after an incident or system failure.

RPO (Recovery Point Objective) (C): RPO defines the maximum tolerable period of data loss for an organization. It's an important factor considered within a DRP, but it's not the overall plan itself. RPO would cover amount of data that is expected to be recovered given a failure while DRP encompasses the whole recovery process necessary to restore the system.

SDLC (Software Development Life Cycle) (D): The SDLC is the process of developing software applications. While secure development practices are important for preventing system failures, the SDLC itself wouldn't directly oversee the restoration process.

An effective DRP should consider factors like RPO, data backup procedures, system redundancy, communication protocols, and testing procedures. By having a well-defined and tested DRP in place, organizations can significantly improve their ability to recover from system failures and minimize disruption to their operations.

16) The vulnerability linked to the installation of software from sources other than the manufacturer's approved software repository is:

D. Side loading

Here's why:

Side loading refers to the practice of installing software applications from unauthorized sources outside of the official channels provided by the device manufacturer or operating system vendor. These sources could be third-party app stores, websites, or physical media.

Risks of side loading:

Unverified software: Software from unapproved sources might be malicious or contain vulnerabilities that haven't been identified or patched.

Lack of security updates: Sideloaded apps might not receive security updates from the developer, leaving them exposed to known exploits.

Compatibility issues: Software downloaded from untrusted sources might not be compatible with the device or operating system, potentially leading to instability or crashes.

Manufacturer repositories: Official app stores and repositories typically have vetting procedures to ensure the software meets certain security and functionality standards before being made available. This reduces the risk of installing malicious or incompatible software.

While the other options are vulnerabilities, they are not directly tied to side loading:

Jailbreaking (A): This refers to removing security restrictions on Apple devices to allow for unauthorized modifications and app installations. It's a specific type of side loading focused on Apple devices.

Memory injection (B): This is a type of attack where malicious code is injected into a program's memory space, allowing the attacker to take control or steal data. It can happen regardless of the software source.

Resource reuse (C): This vulnerability occurs when a program fails to properly clean up resources it has used, potentially allowing an attacker to exploit this for malicious purposes. It's not directly tied to the source of the software.

17) the most likely type of attack taking place is:

A. Password spraying

Here's why:

Password spraying: This attack involves trying a single password against multiple usernames in a short period. The logs show multiple login attempts with the same password ("Spring2023") against different usernames ("jsmith", "administrator", "guest", "cpolk", "fmartin"). This is a typical pattern of password spraying.

Brute-force attack (D): While brute-force attacks also involve multiple login attempts, they typically try many different passwords for a single username. The logs in this case show the same password being used for multiple usernames.

Pass-the-hash (C): This attack involves stealing a user's hashed password and using it to authenticate to a different system. There's no indication of stolen hashed passwords in the logs.

Account forgery (B): This attack involves creating a fake account. The logs show login attempts to existing usernames, not attempts to create new accounts.

Password spraying is a common attack because it can be automated and can succeed if users choose weak passwords or reuse passwords across multiple accounts.

18) Answer: A. Secured zones

Explanation: When assessing the implementation of Zero Trust principles in the data plane, evaluating secured zones is important. Secured zones help define the boundaries within which trust is not automatically granted, aligning with the Zero Trust model's principle of verifying and securing all resources and connections, regardless of location.

Your number one goal is to ensure the area of work is as secure as possible with constant evaluation, & not for the purpose of a specific subject role, or identity.

Threats are already meant to be reduced in a secure area.

19) Out of the options listed, the best solution to enhance security by preventing unauthorized access to internal company resources is:

B. Jump server

Here's why:

Jump server: This is a secure server specifically configured to allow authorized users access to other servers on the network. It acts as an intermediary, adding an extra layer of security and control. Users would first connect to the jump server using their credentials and then be granted access to internal resources based on pre-defined permissions. This creates a more secure approach compared to directly accessing internal servers.

The other options have limitations for this purpose:

RDP server (A): While RDP (Remote Desktop Protocol) can be used for remote access, it's a protocol, not a security solution. By itself, it wouldn't prevent unauthorized access.

Proxy server (C): Proxy servers can be used for various purposes, but they don't inherently restrict access to internal resources. They might forward traffic but wouldn't typically control user access permissions.

Hypervisor (D): Hypervisors are used to manage virtual machines, not directly for controlling user access to internal resources.

20) The best search string to block non-encrypted websites using a web filter is:

B. http://

Here's why:

http://: This identifies URLs that begin with the standard HTTP protocol, which transmits data in plain text. By blocking http://, the filter would prevent users from accessing websites that don't use HTTPS (which encrypts communication).

The other options wouldn't effectively block non-encrypted websites:

encryption=off (A): This string might not be reliable. Not all non-encrypted websites will have "encryption=off" in the URL.

www.*.com (C): This string would block all websites that start with "www." and end with ".com", regardless of encryption. It would also block potentially legitimate https://www. websites.

:443 (D):* This string would block port 443, which is the standard port for HTTPS traffic. This would prevent access to even encrypted websites.

While using http:// as the search string might not capture every single non-encrypted website (some might use non-standard ports), it's the most effective and targeted approach with minimal disruption to legitimate HTTPS traffic.

21) The correct firewall rule to block the malicious IP address 10.1.4.9 from accessing the organization's network is:

B. access-list inbound deny ip source 10.1.4.9/32 destination 0.0.0.0/0

Here's a breakdown of the rule:

access-list inbound: This specifies that the rule applies to inbound traffic entering the network.

deny: This action keyword indicates that the rule will block traffic matching the criteria.

Ip source 10.1.4.9/32: This defines the source IP address to be blocked. The "/32" indicates the entire subnet of 10.1.4.9 (a single IP address).

destination 0.0.0.0/0: This specifies the destination for the blocked traffic. "0.0.0.0/0" represents any IP address, effectively blocking all attempts from 10.1.4.9 to reach any device within the organization's network.

Let's analyze why the other options are incorrect:

A. access-list inbound deny ip source 0.0.0.0/0 destination 10.1.4.9/32: This rule would block all inbound traffic regardless of source IP, essentially shutting down the entire network.

C. access-list inbound permit ip source 10.1.4.9/32 destination 0.0.0.0/0: This rule would allow traffic from 10.1.4.9 to reach any device on the network, which is the opposite of the desired outcome.

D. access-list inbound permit ip source 0.0.0.0/0 destination 10.1.4.9/32: This rule would allow all inbound traffic to reach the specific IP address 10.1.4.9, which wouldn't be secure.

By implementing rule B, the security analyst effectively blocks traffic originating from the malicious IP address, helping to mitigate the security incident.

22) The most secure method for granting administrative access with minimal traffic through the security boundary is:

A. Implementing a bastion host

Here's why:

Bastion host (jump server): This is a dedicated server specifically configured for secure remote access to internal resources. Users would first connect to the bastion host with multi-factor authentication and then access internal systems through the bastion host with additional authorization checks. This keeps the attack surface of internal resources minimal by not exposing them directly to the internet.

The other options have limitations for this purpose:

Perimeter network (B): While perimeter networks can be a security layer, they don't directly address the need for secure administrative access. They might manage overall network traffic flow but wouldn't necessarily control access to internal resources with minimal traffic exposure.

Web application firewall (WAF) (C): WAFs are designed to protect web applications from attacks, not specifically for granting administrative access.

Single sign-on (SSO) (D): While SSO simplifies login processes, it doesn't inherently restrict traffic through the security boundary. It could be used in conjunction with a bastion host for access management, but it's not the primary solution for this scenario.

By using a bastion host, the company can provide secure administrative access while minimizing the attack surface of internal resources on the internet.

23) The most suitable log source for the analyst to investigate the executable running on the employee's laptop is:

D. Endpoint

Here's why:

Endpoint logs: These logs specifically record activity on individual devices, including endpoints like laptops. They typically contain detailed information about processes running on the machine, including executable names, timestamps, and potentially associated user accounts. This data would be crucial for identifying the suspicious executable in question.

To further clarify, endpoint logs are stored on the actual device so the data their looking for should be in endpoint logs.

The other log sources might not provide the necessary details:

Application logs (A): These logs might capture application-specific events, but they wouldn't necessarily provide comprehensive information about all executables running on the system.

IPS/IDS logs (B): Intrusion Prevention/Detection System logs focus on network traffic and potential security incidents. While they might indicate suspicious network activity, they might not pinpoint the specific executable involved.

Network logs (C): Network logs track traffic across the network, but they wouldn't have details about specific executables running on individual devices like laptops.

By analyzing endpoint logs, the security analyst can gain valuable insights into the employee's laptop activity and identify the suspicious executable for further investigation. This could involve checking the file hash against known malware databases or analyzing the executable's behavior for malicious actions.

24) The most appropriate action for the security analyst in this scenario is:

D. Threat hunting

Here's why:

Threat hunting: This is a proactive approach where security analysts actively search for indicators of compromise (IOCs) and suspicious activity within a network, even before alerts are triggered. Since SIEM alerts haven't been configured yet, threat hunting would be the best way to identify the new infiltration method.

The other options are not as suitable in this context:

Digital forensics (A): This involves preserving and analyzing digital evidence after a security incident has already occurred. It wouldn't be the first step for identifying ongoing infiltration.

E-discovery (B): This is a legal process for identifying and collecting electronically stored information (ESI) relevant to a legal case. It wouldn't be the primary focus for investigating a new network infiltration method.

Incident response (C): Incident response is a structured process for containing, eradicating, and recovering from a security incident after it has been identified. While it would be part of the overall response after the analyst identifies the infiltration method, it's not the initial proactive approach.

In this scenario, threat hunting allows the security analyst to be proactive and potentially discover the new infiltration method before it causes significant damage. Once the method is identified, the security operations team can implement incident response procedures to address the threat.

25) The correct answer is: B. Transfer

Here's why:

Accept: This strategy involves acknowledging the risk and its potential impact but choosing not to take any action. Since the company is buying insurance, they are not simply accepting the risk.

Transfer: This strategy involves shifting the financial burden or responsibility for the risk to another party. By purchasing cyber insurance, the company is transferring the potential financial losses from cyber incidents to the insurance provider. This is the most fitting option.

Mitigate: This strategy involves taking steps to reduce the likelihood or impact of a risk. While cyber insurance can indirectly help with mitigation by prompting better security practices to qualify for coverage, directly purchasing insurance focuses on transferring the financial burden, not reducing the risk itself.

Avoid: This strategy involves eliminating the risk altogether.

Purchasing cyber insurance doesn't eliminate the possibility of cyber-attacks, so this doesn't apply.

In conclusion, buying cyber insurance is a risk transfer strategy because it shifts the financial responsibility for cyber incidents to the insurance company.

Note:

Transfer: Transferring a risk involves shifting some or all of the risk to another party, such as an insurance provider, through contractual agreements or financial arrangements. If the company purchases cyber insurance to address items listed on the risk register, it represents a risk transfer strategy. The company is transferring the financial burden of potential cyber incidents to the insurance provider, who will compensate the company for covered losses.

Given the scenario described, the strategy represented by the company's purchase of cyber insurance to address items listed on the risk register is Transfer. The company is transferring some of the financial consequences of potential cyber incidents to the insurance provider through the purchase of insurance coverage.

26) The most suitable encryption technique for securing data on employee laptops is:

C. Full disk

Here's a breakdown of why the other options wouldn't be ideal:

Partition: Partitioning a disk simply divides the storage space into logical sections. While you could encrypt individual partitions, full disk encryption offers a more comprehensive solution.

Asymmetric: Asymmetric encryption is used for secure communication and digital signatures. It's not typically used for directly encrypting entire disks.

Database: Database encryption protects data within a database management system, but it wouldn't be applicable for encrypting the entirety of a laptop's storage.

Full disk encryption ensures all data stored on the laptop's disk, including operating system files, user files, and even temporary data, is encrypted. This makes the data unreadable to anyone without the decryption key, even if they physically remove the hard drive from the laptop. This provides a strong layer of security for sensitive information on employee laptops.

27) The security control type best represented by an acceptable use policy is:

D. Preventive

Here's why:

Detective: Detective controls focus on identifying security incidents after they occur. An acceptable use policy (AUP) doesn't directly detect incidents.

Compensating: Compensating controls aim to reduce the impact of a security incident after it happens. An AUP is not designed to address the aftermath of an incident.

Corrective: Corrective controls aim to fix the root cause of a security incident to prevent similar occurrences. While an AUP can help prevent some security incidents, it's not focused on identifying and fixing specific problems.

Preventive: Preventive controls aim to stop security incidents from happening in the first place. An acceptable use policy outlines expectations for user behavior regarding IT resources, which helps prevent misuse and potential security breaches. This makes it the most fitting category.

An AUP acts as a preventive control by:

Educating users about acceptable and unacceptable IT use.

Setting clear expectations for password management, data security, and internet browsing.

Discouraging actions that could lead to security incidents like malware infection or data breaches.

By outlining these guidelines, an AUP helps prevent security issues before they occur.

28) The security technique the IT manager is setting up is:

D. Least privilege

Here's why:

Hardening: This involves strengthening a system's defenses by removing unnecessary features, configuring security settings, and applying security patches. While the IT manager might be hardening the console access, the specific focus here is on user privileges.

Employee monitoring: This involves tracking employee activity on computers or networks. There's no mention of monitoring in this scenario; the focus is on access control.

Configuration enforcement: This ensures systems are configured according to specific security standards. While relevant, the emphasis here is on the privilege level, not the specific configuration.

Least privilege: This principle dictates that users should only have the minimum level of access needed to perform their tasks. By restricting access to the administrator console to only the IT manager and help desk lead, the IT manager is ensuring that only authorized personnel have the ability to perform administrative tasks.

In this case, the IT manager is following the principle of least privilege to minimize the risk of unauthorized access and potential misuse of the administrator console.

29) The most likely document to include risks, responsible parties, and thresholds is:

C. Risk register

Here's why the other options are less likely:

Risk tolerance: This defines the acceptable level of risk an organization is willing to bear. It wouldn't typically detail specific risks, responsible parties, or thresholds.

Risk transfer: This refers to the strategy of shifting the financial burden or responsibility for a risk to another party. While it might be mentioned in the risk register, the focus wouldn't be on documenting details of each risk.

Risk analysis: This is the process of identifying, assessing, and prioritizing risks. While it would involve considering responsible parties and thresholds, the final documented output is usually the risk register.

Risk register: This is a central document used in risk management to capture identified risks, their likelihood and impact, responsible parties for mitigation, and sometimes thresholds for triggering actions. It's the most comprehensive option for the information you described.

The risk register serves as a central repository for managing all aspects of identified risks, including:

Description of the risk: What is the potential threat?

Likelihood: How probable is it that the risk will occur?

Impact: What are the potential consequences of the risk? (financial, reputational, etc.)

Responsible party: Who is accountable for mitigating the risk?

Thresholds: At what point should action be taken to address the risk? (e.g., severity level)

Therefore, the risk register is the most suitable choice for documenting these elements.

30) The most appropriate guideline for a security administrator to follow when configuring a new set of firewall rules is:

D. Change management procedure

Here's why the other options are less suitable:

Disaster recovery plan: This plan outlines steps to recover IT infrastructure and data after a major disaster. While firewall rule changes could be part of the recovery process, it's not the primary focus when initially configuring them.

Incident response procedure: This procedure outlines how to identify, contain, and recover from a security incident. Similar to disaster recovery, it's not the main concern for setting up new firewall rules.

Business continuity plan: This plan ensures critical business functions can continue despite disruptions. While firewall security is important for business continuity, it's not the sole focus of the plan when configuring new rules.

Change management procedure: This is a formal process

for managing changes to IT systems, including firewalls. It ensures changes are properly documented, reviewed, tested, and approved before implementation. This minimizes the risk of introducing errors or security vulnerabilities with the new firewall rules.

A good change management procedure for firewall rules should involve:

Documentation: Clearly documenting the purpose and impact of the new rules.

Review: Having authorized personnel review the proposed changes for security implications.

Testing: Implementing the changes in a test environment to ensure they function as intended and don't cause unintended consequences.

Approval: Obtaining formal approval before deploying the new rules to the production firewall.

Following a change management procedure helps ensure that new firewall rules are implemented securely and effectively.

31) The correct answer is B. Bug bounty

Here's why the other options are less likely:

Open-source intelligence (OSINT): This involves collecting publicly available information about potential threats. While OSINT can be valuable for security purposes, it's not the same as a program where external individuals test a company's systems for vulnerabilities and receive rewards.

Red team: A red team is a group of security professionals who simulate real-world attacks to test an organization's defenses.

While the company might use a red team internally, a bug bounty program involves external researchers.

Penetration testing: This is a professional service where security experts are hired to identify vulnerabilities in a system. Penetration testing is often more structured and comprehensive than a bug bounty program, where the scope and methodology might be more open-ended.

Bug bounty: A bug bounty program offers rewards to external researchers for finding and reporting vulnerabilities in a company's systems or applications. This is exactly what the company is described as doing in the scenario.

By allowing external individuals to test their application and rewarding them for finding vulnerabilities, the company is implementing a bug bounty program. This approach can be a cost-effective way to identify a wider range of security weaknesses.

32) The most likely threat actor to employ significant financial resources to target critical systems in foreign countries is:

C. Nation-state

Here's why the other options are less likely:

Insider: Insiders may have access to a company's systems but typically wouldn't have the resources to launch large-scale attacks on foreign critical infrastructure.

Unskilled attacker: Unskilled attackers generally lack the resources and sophistication to target critical systems.

Hacktivist: Hacktivists may target critical systems for ideological reasons, but their attacks are often less sophisticated and may not involve significant financial resources.

Nation-states, on the other hand, often have considerable financial backing and advanced capabilities. They may target critical systems in foreign countries for espionage, sabotage, or to disrupt essential services. Nation-states can invest in developing custom exploits, hiring skilled attackers, and maintaining persistent access within target systems.

While other actors can also pose threats, nation-states are generally considered to be the most well-resourced and capable adversaries when it comes to targeting critical systems on a global scale.

33) The answer is: D. SQL injection

Here's why:

Cross-site scripting (XSS): This injects malicious scripts into websites, but these scripts typically run on the client-side (user's browser) and can't directly execute commands on the server that holds the data.

Side loading: This involves installing apps from untrusted sources, but it doesn't necessarily involve an input field for executing commands or manipulating data.

Buffer overflow: This is a memory corruption vulnerability that can be exploited to execute arbitrary code, but it doesn't typically involve an input field for user interaction.

SQL injection: This injects malicious SQL code into a website's form or input field. This injected code can then be executed by the database server, potentially allowing attackers to view, manipulate, or steal data.

SQL injection specifically leverages an input field as a way to introduce malicious code that gets processed by the database server. This allows attackers to potentially:

Read sensitive data: By crafting appropriate SQL queries, attackers can extract confidential information stored in the database.

Modify data: Malicious queries can update or delete data within the database.

Add or remove users: In some cases, attackers might be able to create new user accounts or delete existing ones.

Therefore, SQL injection is the option that best fits the scenario of using an input field to execute commands and manipulate data.

34) The data that research and development employees are most likely to use in their day-to-day work activities is:

B. Intellectual property

Here's why the other options are less likely:

Encrypted: Data can be encrypted at rest or in transit. While encryption is important for security, the type of data itself is a more relevant consideration in this scenario.

Critical: Critical data is any information essential for the organization's operations. While intellectual property (IP) can be critical, the prompt focuses on the specific context of research and development.

Data in transit: This refers to data moving between locations, such as over a network. While R&D might involve data transfer, the core focus is on the type of data they work with.

Intellectual property (IP) encompasses a variety of creations that result from innovation, such as:

Trade secrets (proprietary formulas, inventions)

Copyrights (original creative works)

Patents (exclusive rights to inventions)

Research and development teams are typically involved in creating, developing, and protecting the company's intellectual property. They need to be well-versed in data security practices to safeguard this valuable information.

35) The security benefits provided by these actions are:

A. If a security incident occurs on the device, the correct employee can be notified.

F. Company data can be accounted for when the employee leaves the organization.

Explanation:

Asset inventory stickers linked to employee IDs enable quick identification of the device owner in case of a security incident, facilitating prompt notification and response.

Linking laptops to employee IDs helps in tracking company data stored on the laptops, ensuring that it can be accounted for and properly managed when an employee leaves the organization.

36) The best option to enhance situational and environmental awareness for users transitioning from remote to office work is:

C. Modify the content of recurring training.

Here's why the other options are less suitable:

A. Send out periodic security reminders: While reminders are helpful, they might not be as comprehensive as revising existing training to address the specific challenges of switching work environments.

B. Update the content of new hire documentation: This is important for onboarding new employees, but it wouldn't necessarily target existing staff making the remote-to-office shift.

D. Implement a phishing campaign: Phishing campaigns are used to test user awareness, but they can be disruptive and wouldn't provide the necessary information or guidance for a smooth transition.

Modifying recurring training allows the company to specifically address the security and situational awareness concerns relevant to users moving from remote to office work.

This could include topics like:

Physical security practices in the office (e.g., securing laptops, being mindful of tailgating)

Data security considerations (e.g., using the office network securely, being cautious about using public Wi-Fi)

Importance of good password hygiene and multi-factor authentication (MFA)

Recognizing and reporting suspicious activity or social engineering attempts

Workplace safety protocols and emergency procedures

By incorporating these elements into existing training programs, the company can ensure users are well-prepared and aware of the potential security and situational changes associated with returning to the office environment.

37) The best option for the systems administrator to present data on security incidents to the board of directors is:

D. Dashboard

Here's why the other options are less suitable for board-level reporting:

Packet captures: These capture network traffic data, which can be valuable for forensic analysis but are too granular and technical for a board-level report.

Vulnerability scans: These identify potential weaknesses in systems, but they don't necessarily translate directly to security incidents that have occurred.

Metadata: This refers to data about data, which could be part of the information displayed on a dashboard, but it wouldn't be a complete presentation tool on its own.

A dashboard provides a visual representation of key security metrics related to incidents. It can be customized to display:

Number of security incidents: This is the core information the board member requested.

Incident types: Categorizing incidents by type (e.g., phishing, malware, data breaches) can provide valuable insights.

Severity levels: Highlighting the severity of incidents helps the board understand the potential impact.

Trends over time: Visualizing trends allows the board to see if incident rates are increasing or decreasing.

Resolution times: Reporting on how quickly incidents are resolved demonstrates the effectiveness of security response efforts.

A well-designed dashboard offers a clear, concise, and visually appealing way to communicate security incident data to non-technical audiences like a board of directors.

Note:

Dashboard: A dashboard is a graphical user interface that provides at-a-glance views of key performance indicators (KPIs) and other important metrics. In the context of cybersecurity, a dashboard can be used to present summarized information about security incidents, including the number of incidents, their severity, affected systems, and trends over time. Dashboards can provide a visually appealing and easy-to-understand way to present quarterly incident reports to the board of directors, making them the most suitable option among the choices provided.

Therefore, the systems administrator should use Dashboard to present the quarterly incident reports to the board of directors. A dashboard can effectively summarize incident data and provide a visually appealing presentation format for the board's review.

38) The most likely scenario based on the information provided is:

D. A rootkit was deployed.

Here's why the other options are less likely:

A. The end user changed the file permissions: Changing file permissions wouldn't alter the hash of the cmd.exe file itself.

B. A cryptographic collision was detected: This is extremely unlikely. Cryptographic hashes are designed to prevent collisions, meaning it's very improbable for two different files to have the same hash value.

C. A snapshot of the file system was taken: Taking a snapshot wouldn't modify the actual files on the system, so it wouldn't change the hash of cmd.exe.

Rootkits are malicious software designed to conceal their

presence on a system. A rootkit might modify system files, including executables like cmd.exe, to hide its own activities. This modification would cause the hash of the file to change, triggering the alert from the file integrity monitoring tool.

The fact that no patches have been applied in the past two months further supports the possibility of a rootkit infection. Attackers often exploit unpatched vulnerabilities to gain access to systems and deploy malicious tools like rootkits.

Here are some additional steps the systems administrator should take:

Isolate the affected system: Prevent the potentially compromised system from further network communication to limit potential damage.

Scan for additional malware: Use antivirus and anti-malware tools to identify other malicious software that might be present.

Investigate the system logs: Look for further suspicious activity that might indicate the rootkit's behavior or how it gained access.

Consider forensic analysis: Involve a security specialist to forensically analyze the system to identify the rootkit and determine the best course of action for remediation.

39) In the shared responsibility model for an IaaS cloud environment, the responsibility for securing the company's database falls on the:

A. Client

Here's why the other options are incorrect in the context of IaaS:

B. Third-party vendor: While a third-party vendor might be involved in specific aspects of the environment, the IaaS model places the primary security responsibility on the client.

C. Cloud provider: The cloud provider is responsible for the underlying infrastructure security in IaaS, but not for securing the data or applications running on that infrastructure.

D. DBA (Database Administrator): The DBA plays a crucial role in managing and securing the database, but the overall responsibility for securing the database within the IaaS model rests with the client organization.

In an IaaS model, the cloud provider offers the basic building blocks: compute resources, storage, and networking. The client organization has full control over the operating system, applications, and data stored on the IaaS platform. This includes the responsibility for securing the database itself, such as:

Implementing access controls and permissions for the database.

Configuring security settings for the database software.

Patching and updating the database software.

Backing up the database regularly.

Monitoring the database for suspicious activity.

While the cloud provider may offer some basic security features for the IaaS environment, the onus of securing the database and the data it holds ultimately falls on the client organization.

Note:

The client is the one who is utilizing the data, and would be responsible in the handling, and security of database within the infrastructure provided by the Cloud Provider, or Third-Party Vendor.

40) The most appropriate document for a security company to provide to a client outlining the project details, cost, and timeframe is:

D. SOW (Statement of Work)

Here's why the other options are not the best fit:

A. MSA (Master Service Agreement): This is a broader agreement that outlines the general terms and conditions for ongoing services between a client and a service provider. It wouldn't necessarily detail the specifics of a particular project.

B. SLA (Service Level Agreement): This focuses on the specific metrics used to measure the quality and performance of an ongoing service. While an SLA might be relevant for certain aspects of security services, it wouldn't typically include project details, cost, and timeframe for a one-time project.

C. BPA (Business Process Agreement): This outlines the steps and responsibilities for a specific business process between two organizations. It wouldn't necessarily encompass the details of a security project.

A Statement of Work (SOW) is a detailed document that outlines the scope of work for a specific project. In this case, it would describe the security project requested by the client, including:

Project objectives and deliverables: What is the project aiming to achieve?

Tasks and activities: What specific tasks will be performed by the security company?

Timeline and milestones: When are key project phases expected to be completed?

Costs and fees: How much will the project cost, and what are the payment terms?

Acceptance criteria: How will the successful completion of the project be determined?

By providing a well-defined SOW, the security company can ensure the client has a clear understanding of the project scope, deliverables, timeline, and costs before committing to the project.

41) The technique described is most likely:

D. Salting

Here's why the other options aren't the perfect fit:

Key stretching: This technique is used to slow down brute-force attacks by making it computationally expensive to guess the password. While it can enhance password strength, it doesn't involve adding random characters directly to the password itself.

Tokenization: This replaces sensitive data with a non-sensitive substitute, like a random token. It doesn't directly strengthen the password itself.

Data masking: This hides a portion of the data, but it doesn't alter the underlying password value.

Salting involves adding a random string of characters (the salt) to the password before hashing it. This offers several security benefits:

Unique Hashes: Even if multiple users choose the same password, the addition of a unique salt will result in different hashed values for each user. This makes pre-computed rainbow table attacks infeasible.

Enhanced Security: Since the salt is appended to the password before hashing, it becomes part of the verification process. An attacker cannot crack the password hash without knowing the original password and the corresponding salt.

In the scenario described, appending a random string of 36 characters to the password strengthens it by using salting. This makes it more difficult for attackers to crack the password through techniques like brute-forcing.

The process of adding a random string of characters, referred to as a "salt," to a password before hashing it is called salting. This method enhances password security by ensuring that even if two users have identical passwords, their hashes will differ due to the unique salt, significantly increasing the difficulty for attackers attempting to crack passwords using precomputed tables.

42) The best way for the company to confirm the origin and authenticity of the software is:

A. Validate the code signature.

Here's why the other options are less suitable for verifying the software's origin:

B. Execute the code in a sandbox: While sandboxing can help mitigate risks associated with running unknown code, it doesn't directly verify the software's origin.

C. Search the executable for ASCII strings: Searching for specific strings might be helpful for identifying the software or its functionality, but it wouldn't definitively confirm the vendor.

D. Generate a hash of the files: Generating a hash can be a useful integrity check, but it wouldn't necessarily confirm the origin. The company would need a way to verify the hash against a trusted source from the vendor.

Code signing is a security mechanism where the software vendor digitally signs the software with a cryptographic certificate. This signature can then be validated by the company using the vendor's public key.

Here's how code signing helps confirm origin:

Authenticity: A valid code signature verifies that the software hasn't been tampered with since it was signed by the vendor.

Origin: The signature certificate identifies the vendor who signed the code, confirming its source.

Many software vendors use code signing to ensure the integrity and authenticity of their software. By validating the code signature, the company can have a higher degree of confidence that the software they are deploying is genuine and originated from the intended vendor.

Verifying the code signature is the most effective method to authenticate software, as it guarantees that the software is unaltered and originates from a trusted source. Code signatures, which are digital signatures applied by the software vendor, ensure the integrity and source of the software.

43) The most likely vulnerability exploited in the software is:

A. Memory injection

Here's why the other options are less likely based on the scenario:

Race condition: A race condition occurs when the outcome of a program depends on the unpredictable timing of events. While it can lead to unexpected behavior, it wouldn't necessarily explain the software initiating outbound traffic on random ports.

Side loading: This involves installing apps from untrusted sources. It's not relevant to the existing software exhibiting unusual network behavior.

SQL injection: This vulnerability exploits flaws in how user input is processed by database queries. It wouldn't typically cause the software to generate outbound network traffic.

Memory injection involves injecting malicious code into the memory space of a running program. This malicious code could then manipulate the program's behavior, potentially including:

Network communication: The injected code could establish network connections and send data to unauthorized servers, which aligns with the observed outbound traffic on random ports.

Data theft: The code might steal sensitive information from the server's memory.

System manipulation: The attacker could use the injected code to gain control of the server or perform other malicious actions.

The unusual behavior of the software, typically running local batch jobs without network traffic, suddenly generating outbound traffic on random ports, suggests that some external code is influencing its behavior. Memory injection is a common technique used by attackers to achieve this type of control over a program.

Here are some additional steps the security analyst might take:

Isolate the server: Prevent the compromised server from further communication to limit potential damage.

Examine memory dumps: Analyze memory dumps of the

running process to identify suspicious code or artifacts of the exploit.

Scan for malware: Use antivirus and anti-malware tools to detect any malicious software that might be present.

Patch the software: Update the software to the latest version to address any known vulnerabilities that could have been exploited.

Memory injection vulnerabilities enable the execution of unauthorized code or commands within a software program, resulting in abnormal behavior like generating outbound traffic on random high ports. This problem often stems from software failing to adequately validate or encode input, making it susceptible to exploitation by attackers who can inject malicious code.

44) The most useful approach to determine if the risk transfer cost is lower than the impact of the risk is:

D. ALE (Annualized Loss Expectancy)

Here's why the other options are less suitable for this specific comparison:

ARO (Annualized Rate of Occurrence): This metric tells you how often a risk event is expected to occur in a year. It doesn't directly address the cost or impact of the risk.

RTO (Recovery Time Objective): This defines the acceptable amount of downtime after a disruption. While relevant for certain risks, it doesn't directly translate to cost.

RPO (Recovery Point Objective): This defines the maximum tolerable amount of data loss after an incident. Similar to RTO, it doesn't directly address cost comparison.

SLE (Single Loss Expectancy): This represents the potential financial loss from a single occurrence of the risk event. While a factor in ALE, it doesn't consider the frequency of the event.

ALE (Annualized Loss Expectancy) combines the ARO (annual rate of occurrence) with the SLE (single loss expectancy). It provides a more comprehensive picture of the expected annualized cost associated with a risk.

By calculating the ALE, you can compare it to the potential cost of transferring the risk (e.g., purchasing insurance). If the ALE is higher than the risk transfer cost, then transferring the risk might be a financially beneficial decision.

Here's the formula for ALE:

ALE = ARO x SLE

Therefore, by calculating the ALE, you can make a more informed decision about whether the cost of transferring the risk outweighs the potential financial losses associated with the risk itself.

The Annual Loss Expectancy (ALE) is highly valuable for assessing whether transferring a risk's long-term cost is lower than its impact. ALE is computed by multiplying the Single Loss Expectancy (SLE) by the Annualized Rate of Occurrence (ARO), offering an annual expected loss estimate for a particular risk. This calculation is instrumental in long-term financial planning and risk management determinations.

45) The most likely scenario based on the information provided is:

B. Data is being exfiltrated.

Here's why the other options are less likely:

A. A worm is propagating across the network: While worms can generate network traffic, a sudden burst of DNS queries to external systems wouldn't be the typical behavior of a propagating worm. Worms often exploit vulnerabilities to spread within a network, not necessarily focusing on external DNS requests.

C. A logic bomb is deleting data: Logic bombs are designed to trigger and delete data at a specific time. While the unusual timing (outside business hours) might seem suspicious, logic bombs wouldn't typically generate a high volume of DNS queries. Their focus would be on deleting data locally.

D. Ransomware is encrypting files: Ransomware encrypts files on a system, making them inaccessible. This process typically wouldn't involve a burst of outbound DNS queries.

Data exfiltration involves illegally transferring sensitive data out of an organization. This could be achieved by:

Uploading data to a remote server.

Stealing data and sending it via email.

Using a technique called DNS tunneling to embed data within DNS requests.

An unusually high volume of DNS queries to internet systems outside of business hours suggests a potential attempt to exfiltrate data without being noticed. Attackers might leverage techniques like DNS tunneling to hide their exfiltration activities within seemingly legitimate DNS traffic.

Here are some additional steps the security analyst might take:

Investigate the source of the DNS queries: Identify the specific system or user making the suspicious requests.

Analyze the DNS traffic: Look for patterns or anomalies that might indicate data exfiltration.

Review firewall logs: Check for any unauthorized outbound connections that could be related to the data exfiltration.

Secure the compromised system: Isolate and secure the system suspected of being involved in the data exfiltration.

Data exfiltration is a tactic employed by attackers to illicitly obtain sensitive data from a target system or network by transmitting it through DNS queries and responses. This approach is frequently utilized in advanced persistent threat (APT) attacks, where attackers aim to continually avoid detection within the target environment. An abnormal increase in DNS queries to internet systems during non-business hours is a significant sign of potential data exfiltration. Worms, logic bombs, and ransomware typically do not rely on DNS queries for communication with their command-and-control servers or for executing malicious actions.

Reference:

CompTIA Security+ Study Guide: Exam SYO-701, 9th Edition, page 487; Introduction to DNS Data Exfiltration; Identifying a DNS Exfiltration Attack That Wasn't Real --- This Time.

46) The most important factor for the company to consider when strategizing a disaster recovery site to ensure regulated backup data survives a natural disaster is:

A. Geographic dispersion

Here's why the other options are less relevant in this specific scenario:

Platform diversity: While having backups on different platforms can offer some resilience against platform-specific failures, it wouldn't necessarily address a natural disaster impacting a single location.

Hot site: A hot site is a fully functional replica of the production environment, ready to be used immediately in case of a disaster. However, if the natural disaster affects both the primary site and the geographically close hot site, data loss could still occur.

Load balancing: Load balancing is a technique for distributing workload across multiple servers. It wouldn't directly address data backup and disaster recovery for a natural disaster.

Geographic dispersion involves storing backups in a geographically separate location from the primary site. This ensures that a natural disaster impacting one location wouldn't affect the backup data stored in the geographically dispersed site. This physical separation significantly reduces the risk of total data loss in the event of a natural disaster.

Here are some additional considerations for the company's disaster recovery strategy:

Backup frequency: Regularly backing up data ensures you have a recent copy in case of a disaster.

Data encryption: Encrypting backups adds an extra layer of security in case the backup media is stolen or compromised.

Testing and recovery procedures: Regularly testing disaster recovery procedures helps ensure a smooth and efficient recovery process in the event of a real disaster.

By prioritizing geographic dispersion for backups and

implementing a comprehensive disaster recovery plan, the company can significantly reduce the risk of losing regulated data due to a natural disaster.

Geographic dispersion involves storing backup data in geographically distant locations to reduce the likelihood of a single natural disaster impacting both sites. This approach ensures that the company can recover its regulated data in the event of a disaster at the primary site. Platform diversity, hot site implementation, and load balancing are not directly associated with safeguarding backup data from natural disasters.

Reference:

CompTIA Security+ Study Guide: Exam SY0-701, 9th Edition, page 449; Disaster Recovery Planning: Geographic Diversity.

47) The most appropriate tool for a systems administrator to facilitate the smooth deployment of resources within a cloud provider is:

B. Infrastructure as code (IaC)

Here's why the other options are less relevant for resource deployment in the cloud:

Software as a service (SaaS): This is a cloud-based delivery model where the vendor manages the infrastructure and software application. While SaaS can be beneficial, it wouldn't directly address the management and deployment of resources within a cloud provider.

Internet of Things (IoT): This refers to the network of physical devices embedded with software that collect and exchange data. While IoT devices can be integrated with cloud resources,

IaC specifically focuses on managing and deploying cloud infrastructure components.

Software-defined networking (SDN): This provides programmatic control over network devices and can be beneficial for managing cloud networks. However, IaC has a broader scope, encompassing the entire infrastructure, not just networking.

Infrastructure as code (IaC) allows you to define and provision cloud infrastructure resources using code. This code can be version controlled and reused, making deployments more consistent, repeatable, and less error-prone.

Here are some benefits of using IaC for cloud deployments:

Automation: IaC automates the provisioning and configuration of cloud resources, saving time and effort compared to manual configuration.

Consistency: IaC ensures consistent deployments across different environments, reducing the risk of configuration errors.

Repeatability: IaC scripts can be reused for multiple deployments, making the process more efficient.

Version control: IaC code can be version controlled, allowing you to track changes and rollback to previous configurations if necessary.

By utilizing IaC, systems administrators can streamline the deployment process, ensure consistency, and improve the overall efficiency of managing resources within a cloud environment.

Infrastructure as code (IaC) is an approach that leverages code and automation to manage and provision cloud resources like servers, networks, storage, and applications. IaC enables straightforward deployment, scalability, consistency, and repeatability of cloud environments. It is also a critical element of DevSecOps, which embeds security into the development and operations workflows.

Reference:

CompTIA Security+ Study Guide: Exam SY0-701, 9th Edition, Chapter 6: Cloud and Virtualization Concepts, page 294.

48) The most appropriate option to disable on the routers following a vulnerability scan to strengthen them is:

D. Web-based administration

Here's why the other options are less suitable for enhancing router security:

A. Console access: While console access can be a security risk if not properly secured with strong passwords, it can be a vital tool for troubleshooting and configuration changes. Disabling it completely might hinder legitimate administrative tasks.

B. Routing protocols: Routing protocols are essential for enabling communication between different network segments. Disabling them would disrupt network connectivity.

C. VLANs: VLANs (Virtual LANs) can improve network security by segmenting traffic and limiting broadcast domains. Disabling them could potentially increase the network attack surface.

Web-based administration interfaces on routers can introduce vulnerabilities if not properly secured. Attackers might exploit these vulnerabilities to gain unauthorized access to the router and potentially compromise the network.

Disabling the web-based administration interface can significantly reduce the attack surface of the routers. However, it's important to consider alternative secure methods for managing the routers, such as:

Console access: If console access is enabled, ensure strong passwords are used and consider additional access control mechanisms.

SSH (Secure Shell): SSH is a more secure alternative to traditional telnet access for remote management.

By disabling web-based administration and implementing alternative secure management methods, the security engineer can strengthen the routers and reduce the risk of unauthorized access.

49) The best course of action for the security analyst to identify both the creation date and creator of the suspicious video file is:

D. Query the file's metadata.

Here's why the other options are less suitable:

A. Obtain the file's SHA-256 hash: While a SHA-256 hash can be a unique identifier for the file's content, it wouldn't directly reveal the creation date or creator.

B. Use hexdump on the file's contents: Hexdump displays the file's contents in hexadecimal format. While it might reveal some embedded information within the file itself, it wouldn't be a reliable way to determine the creation date or creator in most video file formats.

C. Check endpoint logs: Endpoint logs might reveal information about when the file was accessed or modified on a specific device, but they wouldn't necessarily tell you the creation date or creator of the file itself.

Video file metadata often includes various details about the file, such as:

Creation date: The date and time the video was created.

Author/Creator: The name of the person or application that created the video.

Camera model: The model of the camera used to record the video (if applicable).

Software used: The software used to edit or encode the video (if applicable).

By examining the file's metadata, the security analyst can potentially identify valuable information about the file's origin and creator, which can be crucial for further investigation.

It's important to note that some video editing tools might allow users to modify or remove metadata. However, it can still be a valuable source of information in many cases.

50) The security bulletin advising a BIOS update is most likely addressing a B. Firmware vulnerability.

Here's why the other options are less likely:

A. Virtualization: While virtualization software can have its own vulnerabilities, a BIOS update wouldn't directly patch those.

C. Application: Application vulnerabilities are typically addressed through patches for the specific software itself, not a BIOS update.

D. Operating system: Operating system vulnerabilities are

patched through updates specific to the operating system, not the BIOS.

The BIOS (Basic Input/Output System) is firmware that provides the foundation for communication between hardware devices and the operating system. Vulnerabilities in the BIOS code could allow attackers to gain control of the system at a very low level, potentially bypassing traditional security measures.

A BIOS update is a patch specifically designed to address vulnerabilities within the BIOS firmware itself. These updates are crucial for maintaining system security and mitigating potential firmware-level exploits.

51) The most suitable option for the systems administrator to restrict user access to the site recovery resource group and implement a simplified access structure is:

A. RBAC (Role-Based Access Control)

Here's why the other options are less aligned with the administrator's goals:

B. ACL (Access Control List): ACLs can be effective for granular access control, but they can also become complex to manage, especially for a large number of users and resources.

C. SAML (Security Assertion Markup Language): SAML is a protocol for secure authentication between a user and an application. While it can be used in conjunction with access control, it's not specifically designed for role-based access within a resource group.

D. GPO (Group Policy Object): GPOs are typically used for managing settings and policies on Windows domain-joined devices. They wouldn't be the most suitable choice for access control within a site recovery resource group, which likely resides in a cloud environment.

RBAC (Role-Based Access Control) simplifies access management by defining roles with specific permissions. Users are assigned roles based on their job functions, and those roles determine what actions they can perform on resources.

Here's how RBAC benefits the scenario:

Simplified Management: RBAC reduces the complexity of managing access control by grouping users with similar needs into roles.

Role-Based Permissions: Permissions are assigned to roles, not individual users, making it easier to manage access changes.

Least Privilege: RBAC encourages the principle of least privilege, ensuring users only have the access they need to perform their jobs.

By implementing RBAC for the site recovery resource group, the administrator can efficiently restrict user access based on roles and responsibilities while maintaining a clear and manageable access structure.

RBAC, or Role-Based Access Control, is a system for restricting access to data and resources based on user roles or responsibilities. This approach simplifies permission management by assigning roles to users and granting access rights to roles, rather than to individual users. RBAC aids in enforcing the principle of least privilege and mitigates the risk of unauthorized access or data breaches. The other options are less appropriate for the scenario compared to RBAC, as they either do not restrict access based on responsibilities or do not employ a simplified format.

Reference:

CompTIA Security+ Study Guide: Exam SY0-701, 9th Edition, page 1331

52) The scenario described most likely indicates a D. Reflected denial of service (DoS) attack targeting the DNS server.

Here's why the other options are less likely:

A. Concurrent session usage: While a high number of concurrent user sessions could increase resource usage, it wouldn't necessarily explain the low CPU, disk, and memory usage observed on the DNS server.

B. Secure DNS cryptographic downgrade: Downgrading the cryptographic protocol might impact security but wouldn't directly lead to overwhelming network traffic.

C. On-path resource consumption: On-path resource consumption refers to resources consumed by network devices along the data path. While this could be an issue, the information provided focuses on the low resource usage on the DNS server itself.

Reflected DoS attack: This type of attack exploits vulnerable DNS servers to amplify traffic directed at a target. Here's how it works in this scenario:

Attacker sends Spoofed Requests: The attacker sends a large volume of DNS requests to the victim's DNS server, spoofing the source IP address to be the target website's IP address.

DNS Server Responds: The compromised DNS server, unaware of the spoofed source, sends legitimate DNS responses to the spoofed IP address (which is actually the target website).

Target Overwhelmed: The target website receives a massive influx of DNS responses, overwhelming its resources and potentially making it unavailable to legitimate users.

Low Resource Usage on DNS Server: The key point is the low resource usage on the DNS server itself. This suggests the server is functioning normally and processing the spoofed requests. The overwhelming network traffic originates from the attacker and is directed at the target website, not the DNS server itself.

Network Logs: The network logs showing only a small number of outbound queries further support this scenario. The DNS server is responding to a large volume of spoofed requests, but those requests are initiated by the attacker, not legitimate users within the company.

By recognizing the signs of a reflected DoS attack, the security analyst can take steps to mitigate the attack and protect the target website.

A reflected denial of service (RDoS) attack is a form of DDoS attack that leverages spoofed source IP addresses to direct requests to a third-party server, which then forwards responses to the victim server. The attacker exploits the difference in size between the request and the response to amplify the volume of traffic directed at the victim server. Additionally, the attacker conceals their identity by employing the victim's IP address as the source. In a RDoS attack targeting DNS servers, the attacker sends falsified DNS queries that produce sizable DNS responses. This inundates the network interface of the DNS server and obstructs its ability to handle legitimate requests from end users.

Reference:

CompTIA Security+ Study Guide: Exam SY0-701, 9th Edition, page 215-2161

53) The most suitable solution to address the organization's scalability challenges with remote work is:

A. Deploying a SASE solution to remote employees.

Here's why the other options are less aligned with all the objectives:

B. Building a load-balanced VPN solution with redundant internet: This would improve scalability for VPN traffic, but it wouldn't necessarily minimize overall traffic or provide built-in monitoring of remote employee internet traffic.

C. Purchasing a low-cost SD-WAN solution for VPN traffic: SD-WAN (Software-Defined Wide Area Network) can optimize traffic flow, but it wouldn't necessarily provide encryption or internet traffic monitoring for remote employees.

D. Using a cloud provider to create additional VPN concentrators: While adding more VPN concentrators might increase capacity, it wouldn't directly minimize traffic or offer the additional functionalities of monitoring and encryption.

SASE (Secure Access Service Edge) combines cloud-delivered security functions with WAN capabilities. Here's how it meets the organization's needs:

Traffic Minimization: SASE solutions can include SWG (Secure Web Gateway) functionality, which can filter and optimize traffic flow, potentially reducing the overall volume of data traversing the VPN and internet circuit.

Encrypted Tunnel Access: SASE solutions typically provide secure access to the data center through encrypted tunnels.

Remote User Monitoring: Some SASE solutions offer features for monitoring and filtering internet traffic used by remote employees.

By deploying a SASE solution, the organization can address all its objectives:

Minimize traffic on the VPN and internet circuit through traffic filtering and optimization.

Ensure encrypted tunnel access to the data center for remote employees.

Monitor remote employee internet traffic for security and policy compliance purposes.

It's important to note that not all SASE solutions offer all functionalities. The organization should evaluate different SASE offerings to ensure it meets their specific needs for traffic minimization, encryption, and internet traffic monitoring.

SASE, which stands for Secure Access Service Edge, is a cloud-based service that integrates network and security functions into a unified solution. It can aid in reducing traffic on the VPN and internet circuit by delivering secure and optimized access to the data center and cloud applications for remote employees. Additionally, SASE can monitor and enforce security policies on remote employee internet traffic, irrespective of their location or device. Compared to traditional VPN solutions, SASE offers benefits like cost reduction, enhanced performance, scalability, and flexibility.

Reference:

CompTIA Security+ Study Guide: Exam SY0-701, 9th Edition, page 457-4581

54) The most likely way to prevent unexpected logins to the remote management interface using the local administrator account of the VPN appliance is:

B. Changing the default password

Here's why the other options are less effective in this scenario:

A. Using least privilege: This principle is generally a good security practice, but it wouldn't directly address the use of a default password on the local administrator account. Least privilege would typically involve assigning users with the minimum permissions they need to perform their jobs, but for the VPN appliance itself, it wouldn't eliminate the inherent risk of a default password.

C. Assigning individual user IDs: While assigning individual user IDs is a good practice for user accountability, it wouldn't necessarily prevent someone from exploiting a weak default password for the local administrator account.

D. Reviewing logs more frequently: Regularly reviewing logs is important for security purposes, but it wouldn't prevent the initial unauthorized access from happening. You might identify the unexpected login after the fact, but it wouldn't stop it from occurring in the first place.

Default passwords are a significant security risk. Attackers often target devices with known default credentials in hopes of gaining unauthorized access.

Changing the default password for the local administrator account on the VPN appliance to a strong, unique password significantly reduces the risk of unauthorized logins. This is a simple but crucial security measure that should be implemented during the initial setup of the appliance.

Here are some additional security recommendations for VPN appliances:

Disable unused remote access protocols.

Enable multi-factor authentication (MFA) for remote access.

Keep the VPN appliance software up to date with the latest security patches.

Segment the network to limit access to the VPN appliance management interface.

By following these security best practices, organizations can significantly reduce the risk of unauthorized access to their VPN appliances.

Changing the default password for the local administrator account on a VPN appliance is a fundamental security measure that could have likely prevented the unexpected login to the remote management interface. Default passwords are frequently simple to guess or publicly accessible, making them vulnerable to unauthorized access by attackers. Changing the default password to a strong and unique one helps mitigate the risk of brute-force attacks and credential theft. While utilizing least privilege, assigning individual user IDs, and reviewing logs more frequently are all good security practices, they are not as effective as changing the default password in preventing the unexpected login.

Reference:

CompTIA Security+ Study Guide: Exam SY0-701, 9th Edition, page 116; Local Admin Accounts - Security Risks and Best Practices (Part 1)

55) The document that likely includes an estimate about the number of hours required to complete a penetration testing engagement with a vendor is the:

A. SOW (Statement of Work)

Here's why the other options are less likely to contain this information:

B. BPA (Business Process Analysis): A BPA focuses on analyzing and improving an organization's internal business processes. It wouldn't typically specify details about a penetration test with a vendor.

C. SLA (Service Level Agreement): An SLA outlines the expected service levels for an ongoing service. While it might mention penetration testing as a service, it wouldn't delve into the specifics of a single engagement, including the estimated time.

D. NDA (Non-Disclosure Agreement): An NDA ensures confidentiality of sensitive information. It wouldn't contain details about the scope or timeline of a penetration test.

SOW (Statement of Work) is a document that outlines the details of a project or engagement between a company and a vendor. In the context of a penetration test, the SOW would typically include:

Scope of the test: What systems and applications will be included in the testing.

Methodology: The techniques and tools that will be used during the testing.

Deliverables: The reports and findings that will be provided by the vendor after the test.

Timeline: An estimated timeframe for completing the

engagement, often including the number of hours or days required.

By including an estimated number of hours in the SOW, both the company and the vendor have a clear understanding of the expected time commitment for the penetration test. This helps with resource allocation, budgeting, and project planning.

A statement of work (SOW) is a document outlining the scope, objectives, deliverables, timeline, and costs of a project or service. It typically includes an estimated number of hours required to complete the engagement, as well as the roles and responsibilities of involved parties. The SOW is commonly used in penetration testing projects to ensure both client and vendor have a clear understanding of expectations and project execution. While a business partnership agreement (BPA), a service level agreement (SLA), and a non-disclosure agreement (NDA) may be relevant to a penetration testing project, they do not provide an estimate of the number of hours needed for the engagement.

Reference:

CompTIA Security+ Study Guide: Exam SY0-701, 9th Edition, page 492; What to Look for in a Penetration Testing Statement of Work?

56) The team that integrates offensive and defensive testing methods to safeguard an organization's critical systems is:

C. Purple

Here's why the other options are not the right answer:

A. Red: Red teams are also known as offensive security

teams. They focus on simulating real-world attacks to identify vulnerabilities in an organization's security posture.

B. Blue: Blue teams are also known as defensive security teams. They focus on monitoring, detecting, and responding to security threats and incidents.

D. Yellow: Yellow teams are not a standard term in cybersecurity.

Purple teams combine the skills and approaches of both red and blue teams. They work collaboratively to identify and address security weaknesses. Here are some key aspects of purple teaming:

Shared knowledge: Red and blue teams share information and insights throughout the testing process.

Continuous improvement: Purple teaming fosters a culture of continuous improvement, where learnings from testing are used to enhance the organization's overall security posture.

Proactive approach: Purple teaming goes beyond traditional red and blue teaming by focusing on proactive prevention and mitigation strategies.

By integrating offensive and defensive testing methods, purple teams provide a more comprehensive assessment of an organization's security posture and help them better prepare for real-world cyberattacks.

The Purple team is not a standalone entity but a collaboration between the Red team, responsible for offensive testing, and the Blue team, responsible for defensive testing, to enhance the organization's security posture. The Purple team integrates defensive tactics and controls from the Blue team with threats and vulnerabilities identified by the Red team to improve overall security. The Red team simulates attacks and exploits vulnerabilities, while the Blue team monitors and defends against real and simulated threats. The Yellow team, on the other hand, develops software solutions, scripts, and programs used by the Blue team in security testing. Red, blue, and yellow are other teams involved in security testing, but they do not integrate offensive and defensive techniques like the Purple team does.

Reference:

CompTIA Security+ Study Guide: Exam SY0-701, 9th Edition, page 1331; Penetration Testing: Understanding Red, Blue, & Purple Teams3

57) The most appropriate risk management strategy for the enterprise to prioritize initially, considering a crucial legacy application with unimplemented preventive controls, is:

A. Mitigate

Here's why the other options are less suitable for this scenario:

B. Accept: Accepting the risk without any mitigation efforts wouldn't be ideal for a critical business application, especially with missing preventive controls.

C. Transfer: Transferring the risk (e.g., through insurance) might be an option in the long run, but it wouldn't address the immediate need to reduce the risk associated with the unimplemented controls.

D. Avoid: Avoiding the application altogether might not be feasible if it's crucial for business operations.

Mitigate focuses on reducing the likelihood or impact of the risk. In this scenario, the enterprise should prioritize implementing preventive controls for the legacy application. Here are some examples of mitigation strategies:

Implement access controls to restrict unauthorized access to the application.

Patch vulnerabilities in the application software.

Implement intrusion detection/prevention systems (IDS/IPS) to monitor for and block malicious activity.

Back up the application data regularly to ensure recovery in case of a security incident.

By focusing on mitigation first, the enterprise can significantly reduce the risk associated with the legacy application while they explore alternative solutions like modernization or replacement in the long term.

Here's a breakdown of the risk management strategies in the context of this scenario:

Mitigate: Prioritize by implementing preventive controls to reduce the risk.

Accept: Not ideal for a critical application with missing controls.

Transfer: Might be considered later, but doesn't address immediate risk.

Avoid: Potentially impractical if the application is crucial for business.

The mitigate risk management strategy involves reducing the likelihood or impact of a risk. If a legacy application is crucial to business operations and some preventive controls are yet to be implemented, the enterprise should prioritize the mitigate strategy to address existing vulnerabilities and gaps in the application. This may include applying patches, updates, or configuration changes to the application, or adding additional layers of security controls around it. While accept, transfer, and avoid are other risk management strategies, they are not the most suitable options in this scenario. Accept entails acknowledging the risk and its consequences without taking action. Transfer involves shifting the risk to a third party, like an insurance company or a vendor. Avoid means eliminating the risk by removing the source or changing the process. These strategies may not be practical or desirable for a critical legacy application lacking preventive controls.

Reference:

CompTIA Security+ Study Guide: Exam SY0-701, 9th Edition, page 1221; A Risk-Based Framework for Legacy System Migration and Deprecation2

58) The incident response activity that ensures evidence is handled properly is:

B. Chain of custody

Here's why the other options are related but address different aspects of evidence handling:

A. E-discovery: E-discovery refers to the process of identifying, collecting, and producing electronically stored information (ESI) for use in legal proceedings. It often relies on a chain of custody to ensure the integrity of the evidence.

C. Legal hold: A legal hold is a process of preserving potentially relevant evidence based on a reasonable anticipation of litigation. It initiates the process, but doesn't necessarily detail how the evidence will be handled.

D. Preservation: Preservation refers to taking steps to prevent the alteration or destruction of potential evidence. It's a crucial step, but chain of custody goes beyond preservation by documenting the movement and handling of evidence.

Chain of custody is a documented record that tracks the movement and handling of evidence from the time it is collected to the time it is presented in court (or used for internal investigations). It ensures the integrity and authenticity of the evidence and helps to demonstrate that it hasn't been tampered with.

Here are some key elements of a chain of custody:

Who collected the evidence?

When and where was the evidence collected?

What is the evidence?

How has the evidence been stored and transported?

Who currently has custody of the evidence?

By maintaining a proper chain of custody, organizations can ensure that evidence collected during an incident response can be used effectively for investigation and potential legal proceedings.

Chain of custody is the procedure for documenting and maintaining the integrity of evidence gathered during an incident response. It includes documenting each person who handled the evidence, the transfer times and dates, and the storage locations. This process guarantees that the evidence is admissible in legal proceedings and can be traced back to its origin. While e-discovery, legal hold, and preservation are related concepts, they do not guarantee the proper handling of evidence.

Reference:

CompTIA Security+ Study Guide: Exam SY0-701, 9th Edition, page 487; NIST SP 800-61: 3.2. Evidence Gathering and Handling

59) The answer is: D. Risk threshold

Here's why the other options are not the highest level of acceptable risk:

A. Risk indicator: This is a signal or data point that suggests potential risk. It doesn't define the level of acceptable risk.

B. Risk level: This categorizes risk based on severity (e.g., high, medium, low). It doesn't necessarily define the specific level an organization is willing to accept.

C. Risk score: This is a numerical value assigned to represent the overall risk based on likelihood and impact. Similar to risk level, it doesn't directly define the acceptable limit.

Risk threshold defines the maximum level of risk that an organization is willing to tolerate before taking action to mitigate it. It acts as a benchmark for risk management decisions. Risks exceeding the threshold require attention and potentially additional controls to reduce them to an acceptable level.

Here's a breakdown of the hierarchy:

Risk indicators: Identify potential threats.

Risk assessment: Analyzes likelihood and impact to determine risk level and score.

Risk threshold: Defines the organization's acceptable risk

tolerance.

Risk management: Implements controls to mitigate risks exceeding the threshold.

By establishing a risk threshold, organizations can prioritize their risk management efforts and ensure they are focusing on the risks that pose the greatest threat to their business objectives.

Risk threshold refers to the maximum level of risk that an organization is prepared to accept for a specific activity or decision. It is also referred to as risk appetite or risk tolerance. The risk threshold aids organizations in prioritizing and allocating resources for risk management. While risk indicator, risk level, and risk score are different methods of measuring or expressing the likelihood and impact of a risk, they do not define the maximum acceptable level of risk.

Reference:

CompTIA Security+ Study Guide: Exam SY0-701, 9th Edition, page 34; Accepting Risk: Definition, How It Works, and Alternatives.

60) The most likely method a company will use to ensure sensitive data at rest is encrypted to make it unreadable is:

C. Encryption

Here's why the other options are less suitable for this specific purpose:

A. Hashing: Hashing creates a unique mathematical value (hash) for the data. While hashing can be used for data integrity purposes, it doesn't encrypt or obfuscate the data itself.

B. Tokenization: Tokenization replaces sensitive data with a substitute value (token) that cannot be easily reversed back to the original data. While it can be a useful security measure, it doesn't necessarily encrypt the data at rest.

D. Segmentation: Segmentation involves dividing a network into smaller segments to isolate sensitive data. While it can improve security, it doesn't directly encrypt the data at rest.

Encryption transforms plain text data into ciphertext using a cryptographic algorithm and a key. This ciphertext is unreadable without the decryption key. Encryption is the most widely used method for protecting sensitive data at rest, ensuring it remains confidential even if someone gains unauthorized access to the storage location.

Here are some common encryption methods used for data at rest:

AES (Advanced Encryption Standard): A popular symmetric encryption algorithm used for a wide range of applications.

TDE (Transparent Data Encryption): A feature that encrypts data at rest on storage devices without user intervention.

By implementing encryption for data at rest, companies can significantly reduce the risk of data breaches and unauthorized access to sensitive information.

Encryption is a technique used to transform data into a format that is unreadable without the appropriate decryption key. It is a highly effective method for protecting data at rest, as it prevents unauthorized access, modification, or theft. Encryption can be applied to various types of data at rest, including block storage, object storage, databases, and archives.

Hashing, tokenization, and segmentation are not used for rendering data at rest unreadable. Hashing is a one-way function that produces a fixed-length output (hash) from an input, making it impossible to retrieve the original input from the hash. Hashing is primarily used for data integrity and authenticity verification, not for encryption.

Tokenization involves replacing sensitive data with non-sensitive substitutes (tokens) that have no inherent value or meaning. Tokenization is used to minimize the exposure and compliance scope of sensitive data, but it does not encrypt the data.

Segmentation is a method of dividing a network or system into smaller, isolated segments, each with different levels of access and security. Segmentation helps reduce the attack surface and contain the impact of a breach, but it does not encrypt data at rest.

Reference:

CompTIA Security+ Study Guide: Exam SY0-701, 9th Edition, pages 77-781; Protecting data at rest - Security Pillar3.

61) The most suitable term to describe the security control of requiring photo ID and access control vestibule for visitors in a secure facility is:

A. Physical

Here's why the other options are less applicable:

B. Managerial: Managerial controls involve policies, procedures, and guidelines established by management to manage security risks. While this might encompass requiring photo IDs and access control procedures, it doesn't directly refer to the physical security measures themselves.

C. Technical: Technical controls involve hardware and software tools used to safeguard systems and data. An access control system could be considered technical, but in this scenario, the emphasis is on the physical barriers and procedures, not the specific technology used.

D. Operational: Operational controls relate to the day-to-day activities performed by personnel to implement security measures. While checking IDs and controlling access are operational activities, the overall category refers to the procedures themselves, not the physical aspects.

Physical security controls involve tangible measures to safeguard physical assets, personnel, and information. In this scenario, both the photo ID requirement and the access control vestibule are physical security measures that deter unauthorized access to the secure facility.

62) The company setting up a SIEM system with weekly log reviews is implementing a C. Detective control.

Here's why the other options are not the best fit:

A. Corrective: Corrective controls address security incidents after they have already occurred. While SIEM can be used for investigating past incidents, the weekly review focuses on proactive detection, not correction.

B. Preventive: Preventive controls aim to stop security incidents from happening in the first place. SIEM can play a role in prevention by identifying potential threats, but the weekly review itself is more focused on identifying ongoing or recent events.

D. Deterrent: Deterrent controls discourage potential attackers from attempting a security breach. SIEM doesn't directly deter attackers, but it can help with faster detection and response, which can reduce the potential benefits of an attack.

Detective controls help identify security incidents or suspicious activity that has already occurred. SIEM systems collect and analyze logs from various security sources, allowing analysts to detect potential threats and investigate further. The weekly review process ensures that the SIEM data is actively monitored for security events.

By implementing a SIEM system and conducting regular log reviews, the company is establishing a detective control to proactively identify and respond to potential security incidents.

A detective control is a security measure that observes and evaluates events to identify and report potential or actual security incidents. A SIEM system serves as an example of a detective control by aggregating, correlating, and analyzing security data from multiple sources, alerting security teams to potential threats. Corrective, preventive, and deterrent controls are alternative security measures that seek to rectify, safeguard against, or dissuade security breaches, respectively.

Reference:

CompTIA Security+ Study Guide: Exam SY0-701, 9th Edition, page 33; What is Security Information and Event Management (SIEM)?

63) The most suitable operating system security measure for the

administrator to implement a password policy change across an enterprise environment quickly is:

B. Pushing GPO update

Here's why the other options are less suitable for this scenario:

A. Deploying PowerShell scripts: While PowerShell scripts can automate tasks, they would need to be created, tested, and deployed to each system individually. This wouldn't be the most efficient method for a large-scale enterprise environment.

C. Enabling PAP (Password Authentication Protocol): PAP is a weak authentication protocol not recommended for secure password management. It wouldn't be a suitable solution for enforcing a strong password policy.

D. Updating EDR profiles: EDR (Endpoint Detection and Response) profiles focus on threat detection and response on individual endpoints. While they might be used for enforcing security policies, they wouldn't be the most efficient way to centrally manage password policy changes across the entire enterprise.

GPO (Group Policy Object): In a Windows domain environment, GPOs are the most efficient way to centrally manage and enforce security policies, including password policies, across a large number of systems. By updating the GPO with the new password policy requirements, the administrator can ensure the changes are automatically applied to all domain-joined systems.

Here are some benefits of using GPOs for password policy enforcement:

Centralized Management: Changes are made in one location (GPO) and automatically applied to all affected systems.

Consistency: Ensures all systems enforce the same password

policy requirements.

Scalability: Efficiently updates password policies across a large number of systems.

By leveraging GPOs, the administrator can achieve a fast and consistent roll-out of the new password policy across the entire enterprise environment.

A Group Policy Object (GPO) is a method for applying configuration settings to computers and users in an Active Directory domain. By pushing a GPO update, the systems administrator can efficiently and consistently enforce the new password policy across all systems in the domain. Deploying PowerShell scripts, enabling PAP, and updating EDR profiles are not the optimal methods for changing the password policy within an enterprise environment.

Reference:

CompTIA Security+ Study Guide: Exam SY0-701, 9th Edition, page 115; Password Policy - Windows Security.

64) Correct answer: A. A full inventory of all hardware and software.

A comprehensive inventory of all hardware and software is crucial for assessing the overall risk to an organization when a new vulnerability is disclosed. This inventory enables the security analyst to pinpoint affected systems and prioritize remediation efforts. Lack of a full inventory may result in overlooking vulnerable systems or misallocation of resources. While documentation of system classifications, a roster of system owners and their departments, and third-party risk assessment documents are valuable for risk management, they alone do not suffice for gauging the impact of a new vulnerability.

Reference:

CompTIA Security+ Study Guide: Exam SY0-701, 9th Edition, page 1221; Risk Assessment and Analysis Methods: Qualitative and Quantitative3.

65) The scenario describes a B. Smishing attack.

Here's why the other options are less likely:

A. Vishing: Vishing attacks involve voice calls impersonating a legitimate entity (like the CEO) to trick the victim into revealing personal information or taking unwanted actions. In this case, the text message indicates a smishing attempt.

C. Pretexting: Pretexting is a broader social engineering tactic where the attacker creates a fake scenario (pretext) to gain the victim's trust and extract information or resources. The smishing message can be seen as a pretext, but the specific method used here is text-based, aligning with smishing.

D. Phishing: Phishing attacks typically involve emails attempting to lure the victim into clicking malicious links or divulging sensitive information. While phishing can occur via SMS, the term "smishing" is specifically used for phishing attacks delivered through SMS (text messages).

Smishing leverages SMS (Short Message Service) to impersonate a trusted source and trick the recipient into taking an undesired action, such as purchasing gift cards in this scenario. The attacker might exploit the urgency or authority associated with the impersonated figure (CEO) to manipulate the recipient.

Smishing is a form of phishing attack that employs text messages or popular messaging apps to deceive victims into clicking on malicious links or divulging personal information. The situation described in the question illustrates a smishing attack utilizing pretexting, a social engineering technique involving impersonation to build trust or gain access. The unfamiliar number pretends to be the company's CEO and requests the employee to buy gift cards, a typical scam strategy. Vishing is akin to smishing but uses phone calls or voicemails, whereas phishing encompasses any email-based attack.

Reference:

CompTIA Security+ Study Guide: Exam SY0-701, 9th Edition, page 771; Smishing vs.Phishing: Understanding the Differences2.

66) A. IPS (Intrusion Prevention System)

Explanation:

An Intrusion Prevention System (IPS) can help mitigate the spread of ransomware by actively monitoring network traffic for malicious activity and blocking it before it can reach vulnerable systems. In this scenario, an IPS could potentially detect the lateral spread of ransomware across the network and take action to prevent it from further compromising systems.

B. IDS (Intrusion Detection System)

An Intrusion Detection System (IDS) is similar to an IPS but does not actively block malicious traffic. Instead, it detects and alerts administrators to potential threats, which they can then investigate and mitigate. While an IDS could help in identifying the ransomware's lateral movement, it would not directly prevent its spread like an IPS would.

C. WAF (Web Application Firewall)

A Web Application Firewall (WAF) is designed to protect web applications from various attacks, including those carried out through phishing links. While a WAF can help protect against certain types of attacks, it is not specifically designed to detect or mitigate ransomware spread across a network.

D. UAT (User Acceptance Testing)

User Acceptance Testing (UAT) is a process used to verify that a system meets its requirements and is acceptable for delivery to end-users. While UAT is an important part of software development and deployment, it is not directly related to mitigating the spread of ransomware in this scenario.

Therefore, the best option for mitigating the spread of ransomware in this scenario would be A. IPS (Intrusion Prevention System), as it can actively monitor and block malicious traffic to prevent further compromise of systems.

67) Out of the options provided, the two most important considerations for the security engineer deploying FDE are:

A. Key escrow: This ensures that there's a backup mechanism for encryption keys in case users forget their passwords or lose access. Without key escrow, data becomes permanently inaccessible.

B. TPM presence: Trusted Platform Module (TPM) is a hardware chip that enhances security by storing encryption keys and performing cryptographic operations. Its presence can improve security and performance of FDE.

Here's why the other options are less critical in this scenario:

C. Digital signatures: While important for digital document verification, it's not directly related to disk encryption.

D. Data tokenization: This replaces sensitive data with random symbols, which wouldn't be applicable for full disk encryption as the entire disk is encrypted.

E. Public key management: This is more relevant for encrypting data in transit (e.g., emails) rather than full disk encryption.

F. Certificate authority linking: This is related to establishing trust in digital certificates, not directly relevant to FDE.

Therefore, focusing on key escrow and TPM presence during FDE deployment is crucial for ensuring data security and accessibility.

68) Correct answer: A. Brute-force attack

A brute-force attack is a method where an attacker systematically tries all possible password or key combinations until the correct one is found. The log file reveals numerous unsuccessful logins attempts within a short timeframe, a hallmark of a brute-force attack. Specifically, the attacker is targeting the Administrator account on the server, as indicated by the log. The presence of event ID 4625 in the log signifies failed login attempts, while the status code 0xC000006A indicates that the username is correct, but the password is incorrect. These are telltale signs of a brute-force attack, serving as indicators of compromise (IoC).

Reference:

CompTIA Security+ Study Guide: Exam SY0-701, 9th Edition,

page 215-216 and 2231.

69) The company is likely employing two access management principles in this scenario:

A. Federation: Since the employee's access to other company websites is based on their intranet profile, it suggests a single sign-on (SSO) system. Federation allows users to authenticate once with their intranet credentials and access various authorized platforms without separate logins for each site. This improves convenience and security by reducing the need for managing multiple passwords.

C. Password complexity: Enforcing complex passwords with a minimum length, character types (letters, numbers, symbols) make it significantly harder to crack passwords through brute-force attacks. This strengthens the security of individual accounts on the intranet.

Here's why the other options are less likely:

B. Identity proofing: This is more relevant during initial user registration to confirm the user's identity.

D. Default password changes: While prompting users to change default passwords is a good practice, it's not the only principle at play here.

E. Password manager: The company might not necessarily be providing a password manager in this scenario.

F. Open authentication: This typically refers to less secure authentication methods and wouldn't be ideal for internal accounts.

Federation is an access management principle enabling users to authenticate once and access various resources or services across different domains or organizations. It relies on a trusted third party to store user credentials and provide them to requested resources or services securely, without exposing them. Password complexity is a security measure that mandates users to create passwords meeting specific criteria, such as length, character types, and uniqueness. This measure helps thwart brute-force attacks, password guessing, and credential stuffing by increasing the complexity of passwords, making them more difficult to crack or guess.

Reference:

CompTIA Security+ Study Guide: Exam SY0-701, 9th Edition, page 308-309 and 312-3131

70) The best security solution for this scenario is:

D. IPS (Intrusion Prevention System)

Here's why:

Targeted attacks: These attacks focus on specific vulnerabilities, suggesting the attackers are likely using known exploits.

Outdated browsers: This creates a vulnerability window that attackers can exploit.

Widely known exploits: These are identifiable patterns that security solutions can leverage.

An IPS is designed to actively monitor and block malicious network traffic based on predefined signatures. In this case, the IPS can be configured to identify and block exploit attempts targeting vulnerabilities in outdated browsers.

Here's why the other options are less suitable:

A. ACL (Access Control List): ACLs define access permissions but wouldn't be effective in identifying and blocking specific exploit attempts.

B. DLP (Data Loss Prevention): DLP focuses on preventing unauthorized data exfiltration, not necessarily blocking network-based attacks.

C. IDS (Intrusion Detection System): While an IDS can detect suspicious activity; it doesn't actively block attacks like an IPS. An IDS could be a good complement to an IPS, providing additional insights into the attack attempts.

An Intrusion Prevention System (IPS) is a security appliance that scrutinizes network traffic and halts or alters malicious packets based on predefined rules or signatures. It serves to thwart attacks exploiting known vulnerabilities in outdated browser versions by identifying and discarding the malicious packets before they reach the intended system. Additionally, an IPS can perform supplementary functions like rate limiting, encryption, or redirection.

Reference:

CompTIA Security+ Study Guide: Exam SY0-701, 9th Edition, Chapter 3: Securing Networks, page 132.

71) The most suitable solution for the company's cloud transition is:

B. CASB (Cloud Access Security Broker)

Here's why CASB aligns with the company's requirements:

Prohibit downloads: CASB solutions often offer data loss prevention (DLP) capabilities that can restrict unauthorized downloads of company applications.

Limit data upload: CASB can monitor and enforce policies on the amount and type of data uploaded to the cloud, preventing unauthorized data exfiltration.

Application visibility: CASB provides insights into cloud application usage across the organization. It can identify sanctioned and unsanctioned apps, helping with application control and potential shadow IT discovery.

While the other options have some overlapping functionalities, CASB offers a more comprehensive solution for cloud security:

A. NGFW (Next-Generation Firewall): An NGFW primarily focuses on securing network traffic and wouldn't directly address application download restrictions, data upload limitations, or cloud application visibility.

C. Application whitelisting: This technique allows only approved applications to run on devices. While effective for on-premise deployments, it wouldn't necessarily address data upload limitations or cloud application visibility.

D. NG-SWG (Next-Generation Secure Web Gateway): Similar to an NGFW, an NG-SWG offers advanced web filtering and security features but might not have the same level of granular control over cloud application usage and data transfer as a CASB.

Therefore, a CASB provides the most comprehensive feature set to meet the company's cloud security needs for application control, data security, and application visibility.

72) Correct answer: B. Sensitive

Explanation:

Sensitive data classification should be used to secure patient data. Sensitive data includes information that, if disclosed, could result in harm to individuals or the organization. Patient data falls into this category due to privacy concerns and the potential consequences of unauthorized access or disclosure.

73) The most suitable solution to address suspicious connections between internal endpoints after a perimeter firewall is in place is:

A. Host-based firewall

Here's why:

Perimeter firewall: This is a first line of defense, typically filtering traffic entering or leaving the network. However, it might not be able to catch malicious activity happening entirely within the network.

Host-based firewall: This software application resides on individual devices and monitors incoming and outgoing traffic on those devices. It can be effective in identifying and blocking suspicious communication between internal endpoints.

Web application firewall (WAF): While WAFs are crucial for securing web applications, they wouldn't necessarily address internal endpoint communication.

Access control list (ACL): ACLs define access permissions but wouldn't be as effective as a host-based firewall in dynamically identifying and blocking suspicious connections within the network.

Application allow list: This technique restricts applications that can run on a device. While valuable for controlling software execution, it wouldn't directly address communication between existing applications or potential malware operating on internal systems.

Therefore, a host-based firewall provides a more targeted approach to securing individual devices and monitoring their network activity, helping to mitigate suspicious connections within the internal network that might bypass the perimeter firewall.

74) Out of the listed options, the security implication the team is most likely to document is:

A. Patch availability

Here's why:

Patch availability: End-of-life (EOL) operating systems no longer receive security patches from the vendor. This leaves the kiosks vulnerable to known and newly discovered exploits, significantly increasing the security risk.

Product software compatibility: While this might be a concern, it's not the most critical implication in this scenario. Newer software might not be compatible with the kiosks, but this wouldn't necessarily create a direct security risk.

Ease of recovery: Recovering from a security incident might be more challenging on an EOL system, but it's not the primary security concern. The focus is on preventing the incident in the first place.

Cost of replacement: The cost of replacing the kiosks is a financial consideration, but it wouldn't be documented as a security implication.

The lack of security patches is the most critical security risk associated with running EOL operating systems. Hackers can exploit these vulnerabilities to gain unauthorized access to the kiosks, steal customer data, or even disrupt kiosk functionality.

75) Out of the options provided, the policy describes:

B. Sanitization

Here's why:

Enumeration: This refers to the process of creating a list of items. While creating a list of hard drives before wiping might be part of the process, it's not the core objective of the policy.

Sanitization: This involves securely wiping a storage device to remove all data, making it unrecoverable. This aligns with the company's policy of ensuring data security before recycling hard drives.

Destruction: While physical destruction is another method for data security, the policy specifically mentions "wiping" which suggests software-based sanitization.

Inventory: Similar to enumeration, inventory management is a separate process that might track company assets, but it's not the core focus of the data security policy.

Therefore, "sanitization" best describes the policy of securely wiping hard drives before disposal.

76) Considering the focus on cost-effectiveness and tolerating a two-day RTO and RPO, the most suitable data center type for this scenario is:

C. Cold

Here's why:

Real-time recovery: This offers the fastest recovery but comes at a significant cost. It wouldn't be ideal for a cost-effective approach.

Hot site: A hot site has fully configured systems ready to take over in case of a disaster. While offering fast recovery, it's also the most expensive option due to maintaining a duplicate infrastructure.

Cold site: This is the most cost-effective option. It has the infrastructure (power, cooling, network connectivity) but no pre-configured servers or data. Setting up the systems and restoring data takes time, resulting in a two-day RTO and RPO, which aligns with the organization's goals.

Warm site: A warm site has some components pre-configured, offering a balance between cost and recovery time. However, it might still be more expensive than a cold site for this scenario where a two-day recovery timeline is acceptable.

Since cost is the primary concern, and the organization can tolerate a two-day downtime, a cold site offers the most cost-effective solution that meets their RTO and RPO requirements.

77) The administrator used a B. Detective control in this scenario.

Here's why:

Preventive controls: These aim to stop security incidents from happening in the first place, such as firewalls, intrusion detection systems (IDS), and data encryption. Examining log files after an attack isn't preventive.

Detective controls: These helps identify security incidents that have already occurred. Analyzing log files to understand the scope and potential cause of a ransomware attack falls under detective controls.

Compensating controls: These attempt to limit the damage after a security incident. While the administrator might use the information from the logs to implement compensating controls (e.g., restoring backups), examining the logs itself is a detective action.

Corrective controls: These address the root cause of a security incident to prevent future occurrences. Analyzing logs can provide valuable insights, but it's the initial investigation and potential security posture adjustments that would be considered corrective actions.

Therefore, examining log files after a security incident is a detective control as it helps identify what happened and potentially how to respond.

78) Correct answer: C. Supply chain vendor

Explanation:

Partnering with a supply chain vendor introduces a risk as it involves integrating third-party services or products into the company's infrastructure. It's essential to vet these vendors thoroughly to ensure they meet security standards and do not introduce vulnerabilities into the system.

79) B. Testing the policy in a non-production environment before enabling the policy in the production network

Explanation:

Testing the policy in a non-production environment allows the technician to identify and resolve any issues before implementing the policy in the production network, thereby preventing the servers from becoming unreachable.

A. Documenting the new policy in a change request and submitting the request to change management: While good practice for tracking changes, it wouldn't directly address the technical problem of the "deny all" rule blocking all traffic.

B. Testing the policy in a non-production environment before enabling the policy in the production network: This is the best course of action! Testing the policy in a separate, controlled environment would have revealed that the "deny all" rule was blocking all traffic, including legitimate connections to the servers.

C. Disabling any intrusion prevention signatures on the 'deny any' policy prior to enabling the new policy: This option wouldn't be relevant. "Deny any" refers to blocking all traffic, not intrusion prevention signatures.

D. Including an 'allow any' policy above the 'deny any' policy: This would effectively bypass all firewall rules, rendering the firewall useless. It's important to have specific "allow" rules for desired traffic before the "deny all" rule to ensure only authorized traffic gets through.

Therefore, the most appropriate action to prevent the issue is B. Testing the policy in a non-production environment before enabling the policy in the production network. This allows for identifying and correcting any configuration mistakes before impacting critical systems in the production network.

80) Out of the listed options, the best practice that provides a defined timeframe for making changes to operational systems is:

B. Scheduled downtime

Here's why:

Impact analysis: While crucial for understanding the potential consequences of a change, it doesn't directly define a timeframe for implementing the change.

Backout plan: This is a critical element for any change, but it focuses on having a rollback strategy in case of issues, not necessarily defining a timeframe for the change itself.

Change management boards: These boards review and approve changes, but they typically wouldn't dictate the specific timeframe for implementing approved changes within the operational window.

Scheduled downtime: This practice involves designating a specific window of time for planned maintenance or system updates. This timeframe allows administrators to make changes with minimal disruption to ongoing operations.

Scheduled downtime helps to:

Improve communication: Users can be informed about the downtime window and plan their work accordingly.

Minimize risk: Changes can be implemented in a controlled environment, reducing the chance of impacting critical systems during business hours.

Facilitate testing: The downtime window allows for thorough testing of the changes before they go into full production.

Therefore, scheduled downtime offers a defined timeframe for making changes to operational systems while ensuring availability and minimizing business impacts.

81) The most fitting description for this penetration test scenario is:

A. Partially known environment

Here's why the other options wouldn't be as accurate:

Unknown environment: In this scenario, the tester wouldn't have any prior knowledge about the device or its configuration.

Integrated: This type of test typically focuses on assessing an entire system or network, not just a single device.

Known environment: While the organization has provided some details, a fully known environment would imply complete knowledge of the device's configuration and potential vulnerabilities.

In a partially known environment penetration test, the tester has some information about the device (e.g., operating system, version) but might not have full access or complete knowledge of its security posture. This is a common scenario where vendors might need to perform targeted testing on specific devices within a network.

82) Out of the provided options, the threat actor the CISO is most likely highlighting in the report is:

D. Organized crime

Here's why the other options are less likely:

Insider threat: This refers to malicious activity from within the organization, whereas RaaS attacks are typically perpetrated by external actors.

Hacktivist: These actors are often motivated by ideology or social change, not financial gain. While some hacktivist groups might use ransomware, it wouldn't be the primary focus in a report about RaaS.

Nation-state: Nation-state actors might use sophisticated

attacks for espionage or disruption, but RaaS is more commonly associated with financially motivated cybercrime groups.

RaaS specifically lowers the barrier to entry for cybercrime, making it easier for organized crime groups to launch ransomware attacks without needing extensive technical expertise. This ease of use and potential for significant financial gain make organized crime a major threat landscape when it comes to RaaS attacks.

In the CISO's report, highlighting the rise of RaaS and its connection to organized crime can help raise awareness among management regarding the evolving threat landscape and the importance of robust cybersecurity measures to defend against financially motivated cyberattacks.

83) Out of the listed options, the most suitable solution for the security architect's needs is:

C. HSMaaS (Hardware Security Module as a Service)

Here's why HSMaaS aligns with the architect's requirements:

Managing encryption keys: HSMaaS offers a centralized platform for managing encryption keys across multiple cloud providers, reducing the administrative burden and complexity.

Minimal latency: HSMaaS providers often have geographically distributed instances to ensure low latency for key access and encryption/decryption operations.

Uniform control: HSMaaS provides a central point of control for key management policies and access, regardless of the data location in the multicloud environment.

Current key integration: Many HSMaaS solutions allow integration with existing encryption keys, avoiding the need to completely replace the organization's key infrastructure.

Let's explore why the other options wouldn't be ideal solutions:

Trusted Platform Module (TPM): TPM is a hardware chip that can store encryption keys on individual devices. While it offers security benefits, it wouldn't provide the centralized management and cloud-agnostic approach the architect needs.

IaaS (Infrastructure as a Service): IaaS is a cloud service model that offers virtualized infrastructure resources. While it can be used to deploy encryption solutions, it wouldn't directly address key management challenges.

PaaS (Platform as a Service): PaaS provides a platform for developing and deploying applications. It might not offer the specific key management functionalities required in this scenario.

Therefore, HSMaaS provides a centralized, secure, and scalable solution for managing encryption keys across a multicloud environment, addressing the security architect's concerns about administrative burden, latency, and uniform control over encryption processes.

84) The best use case for the scenario described is:

B. Orchestration

Here's why orchestration is the most suitable option:

Account creation: Orchestration tools can automate repetitive tasks, including creating user accounts with predefined configurations. This aligns with the administrator's goal of streamlining account creation.

Large number of users: Orchestration excels at handling bulk operations, making it efficient for provisioning accounts for many users at once.

Reduced human error: By automating the process, orchestration minimizes the possibility of errors that might occur during manual account creation.

Let's analyze why the other options wouldn't be the best fit:

Off-the-shelf software: While some software can automate user provisioning, it might not offer the same level of customization and control as orchestration tools.

Baseline: A baseline refers to a standard configuration for a system or software. It wouldn't directly address the task of automating account creation.

Policy enforcement: Policy enforcement tools ensure adherence to security policies. While important, it's not the primary focus here. Orchestration can be used to enforce policies during account creation (e.g., setting strong password requirements).

In conclusion, orchestration provides an automated and efficient way to create numerous user accounts consistently and with minimal human intervention, perfectly aligning with the administrator's goals.

85) Correct answer: B. Non-repudiation

Explanation:

Non-repudiation is the concept that a sender cannot deny sending a message, and a recipient cannot deny receiving it. This attribute allows for the attribution of messages to specific individuals, ensuring accountability and traceability.

86) Here are the two crucial factors to consider when developing a training curriculum for a security awareness program:

C. Threat vectors based on the industry in which the organization operates: Different industries face varying cybersecurity threats. For instance, a financial institution needs to be particularly aware of social engineering scams targeting account information, while a healthcare organization might prioritize training on protecting patient data from unauthorized access. Tailoring the training to address the specific threats relevant to the organization's industry helps employees understand the risks they encounter most often.

E. Cadence and duration of training events: Security awareness training shouldn't be a one-time event. Regular reinforcement through recurring training sessions helps keep cybersecurity best practices top of mind for employees. The optimal cadence and duration will depend on the organization's needs and the complexity of the training material. Shorter, more frequent sessions might be more effective for busy schedules, while deeper dives into specific topics could be offered less frequently.

Here's why the other options are less critical:

A. Channels by which the organization communicates with customers: While understanding communication channels can be helpful for crafting phishing simulations, it's not a core curriculum element.

B. The reporting mechanisms for ethics violations: This information might be relevant for compliance training, but it's not a central focus of security awareness training.

D. Secure software development training for all personnel: This would be more relevant for developers and IT security teams, not necessarily all employees in a security awareness program.

F. Retraining requirements for individuals who fail phishing simulations: While retraining for those who fall victim to simulations can be valuable, it's not the only factor to consider for the overall training program design.

By focusing on industry-specific threats and establishing a regular training cadence, you can create a security awareness program that effectively equips employees to identify and mitigate cybersecurity risks.

87) Out of the listed options, the most suitable solution for protecting data with monitoring and tracing capabilities is:

D. FIM (File Integrity Monitoring)

Here's why FIM is the best fit:

Data protection: FIM detects unauthorized changes to files and directories, alerting administrators to potential security incidents. This helps protect data by identifying suspicious modifications.

Monitoring and tracing: FIM logs changes to files, including timestamps and usernames associated with the modifications. This allows administrators to monitor file integrity and trace any changes back to the responsible user or process.

Let's explore why the other options wouldn't be ideal solutions:

SPF (Sender Policy Framework): While SPF helps prevent email spoofing, it wouldn't directly address file integrity or monitor modifications.

GPO (Group Policy Object): GPOs are used to manage settings and configurations on Windows systems. They can be helpful for enforcing security policies but wouldn't provide the specific file monitoring and tracing capabilities required in this scenario.

NAC (Network Access Control): NAC focuses on controlling network access for devices. While it can be a valuable security tool, it wouldn't provide file-level monitoring or change detection.

Therefore, FIM offers the most comprehensive solution for protecting data by detecting unauthorized modifications and providing audit trails for tracing changes within the environment.

88) Out of the listed options, the most secure method for a security consultant to remotely access a client's environment is:

C. IPSec (IP Security)

Here's why IPSec is the best choice:

Secure communication: IPSec encrypts data traffic at the network layer (IP), ensuring confidentiality and integrity of the data transmitted between the consultant's device and the client's network.

Let's see why the other options wouldn't be ideal for secure remote access:

EAP (Extensible Authentication Protocol): EAP is an authentication framework, but it wouldn't necessarily encrypt the data traffic itself.

DHCP (Dynamic Host Configuration Protocol): DHCP assigns IP addresses to devices on a network. While important for network connectivity, it doesn't provide a secure remote access solution.

NAT (Network Address Translation): NAT translates IP addresses between private and public networks. It wouldn't directly provide secure remote access functionality.

IPSec, with its encryption capabilities, offers a secure tunnel for the consultant to access the client's environment remotely.

Here are some additional security considerations for remote access:

Multi-factor authentication: Implementing multi-factor authentication adds an extra layer of security beyond just password protection.

Access controls: Granting the consultant least privilege access permissions minimize the potential impact in case of unauthorized access.

VPN (Virtual Private Network): While not explicitly mentioned in the options, a VPN can leverage IPSec to create a secure remote access tunnel.

89) The actions taken by the organization best describe D. Compensating controls.

Here's why:

Exception: This refers to an allowed deviation from a security policy. While deactivating unnecessary services might be considered an exception, it's not the main focus here.

Segmentation: This involves dividing a network into smaller segments to limit the blast radius of a security incident. While a firewall can contribute to segmentation, it's not the primary focus in this scenario.

Risk transfer: This involves shifting the financial responsibility for a risk to another party (e.g., insurance). Deactivating services and installing a firewall are actions taken by the organization itself, not a risk transfer.

Compensating controls: These are implemented to address

weaknesses in existing controls or mitigate risks that cannot be entirely eliminated. In this scenario, the legacy system might have inherent vulnerabilities due to its age. Disabling unnecessary services reduces the attack surface, and the firewall adds an extra layer of protection. These actions are implemented to compensate for the potential security weaknesses of the legacy system.

By deactivating unnecessary services and installing a firewall, the organization is putting in place compensating controls to mitigate the security risks associated with the legacy system. This helps to improve the overall security posture even though the legacy system itself might not be easily upgraded or replaced.

90) The vulnerability the organization is most likely addressing by prohibiting mobile OS alterations is:

C. Jailbreaking (or Rooting for Android devices)

Here's why:

Cross-site scripting (XSS): This vulnerability exists in web applications and wouldn't be directly related to modifying a mobile OS.

Buffer overflow: This is a programming vulnerability that can be exploited to execute malicious code. While it could be a theoretical risk, it's not the primary concern for an AUP focused on user actions.

Jailbreaking: This process removes restrictions imposed by the device manufacturer, allowing users to install unauthorized apps and modify system settings. This increases the attack surface of the device and makes it more vulnerable to malware or other security threats.

Sideloading: This refers to installing apps from sources other than the official app store. While it can be risky, it doesn't necessarily involve modifying the underlying operating system. Jailbreaking is often a prerequisite for extensive sideloading of apps.

By prohibiting alterations to the mobile OS, the organization aims to prevent jailbreaking and the associated security risks. This includes:

Loss of security patches: Unauthorized modifications might prevent users from installing critical security updates for the operating system.

Exposure to malware: Jailbroken devices can be more susceptible to malware attacks through untrusted app repositories.

Data breaches: Jailbreaking tools or unauthorized apps might have vulnerabilities that could lead to data breaches on the device.

Therefore, the AUP amendment focuses on mitigating the security risks associated with jailbreaking by preventing employees from modifying the mobile OS.

PRACTICE TEST II

1) Users at a company are reporting an inability to access the URL for a new retail website, as it is classified as gambling and is being blocked. Which of the following changes would allow users to access the site?

A. Creating a firewall rule to allow HTTPS traffic.

B. Configuring the IPS to allow shopping.

C. Tuning the DLP rule that detects credit card data.

D. Updating the categorization in the content filter.

2) Which of the following explains why conducting root cause analysis is important in incident response?

A. To gather loCs for the investigation.

B. To discover which systems have been affected.

C. To eradicate any trace of malware on the network.

D. To prevent future incidents of the same nature.

3) Which of the following is utilized to verify a certificate when it is presented to a user?

A. OCSP

B. CSR

C. CA

D. CRC

4) A recently discovered network access vulnerability has been identified in the operating system of legacy IoT devices. Which of the following would best mitigate this vulnerability quickly?

A. Insurance

B. Patching

C. Segmentation

D. Replacement

5) During an investigation, an incident response team seeks to ascertain the origin of an incident. Which of the following incident response activities describes this process?

A. Analysis

B. Lessons learned

C. Detection

D. Containment

6) A company is creating a critical system for the government and storing project information on a file share. Which of the following describes how this data will most likely be classified? (Select two).

A. Private

B. Confidential

C. Public

D. Operational

E. Urgent

F. Restricted

7) What is the most probable result if a large bank does not pass an internal PCI DSS compliance assessment?

A. Audit findings

B. Sanctions

C. Fines

D. Reputation damage

8) What is the optimal method for consistently checking daily whether security settings on servers have been altered?

A. Manual audit

B. Attestation

C. Compliance checklist

D. Automation

9) What has been enacted when a host-based firewall on a legacy Linux system permits connections solely from specific internal IP addresses?

A. Compensating control

B. Network segmentation

C. Transfer of risk

D. SNMP traps

10) A certificate vendor has informed a company that certificates that were recently invalidated may need to be updated. Which of the following methods should a security administrator employ to ascertain if the certificates installed on the company's machines require updating?

A. SCEP

B. OCSP

C. CSR

D. CRL

11) A security manager has developed new documentation to be used in response to different types of security incidents. Which of the following is the next step the manager should take?

A. Set the maximum data retention policy.

B. Securely store the documents on an air-gapped network.

C. Review the documents' data classification policy.

D. Conduct a tabletop exercise with the team.

12) Which authentication framework, primarily used in

wireless networks and Point-to-Point connections, supports multiple authentication methods?

A. Simple Network Management Protocol (SNMP)

B. Protected Extensible Authentication Protocol (PEAP)

C. Extensible Authentication Protocol (EAP)

D. Lightweight Extensible Authentication Protocol (LEAP)

13) A recent malware outbreak affected a subnet, with many PCs experiencing successful rootkit installations. This ensured persistence of the malware, making remediation efforts ineffective. Which of the following would best detect the presence of a rootkit in the future?

A. FDE

B. NIDS

C. EDR

D. DLP

14) Following a security incident, a systems administrator requests the company to purchase a Network Access Control (NAC) platform. Which of the following attack surfaces is the systems administrator trying to protect?

A. Bluetooth

B. Wired

C. NFC

D. SCADA

15) A company has recently installed a new IoT device on their network. During a security assessment, it was discovered that the device is still configured with default credentials. Which of the following actions is the BEST immediate step to mitigate the potential exploitation of this device?

A. Conduct a thorough vulnerability scan of the device to find potential weaknesses.

B. Update the IoT device firmware to the latest version available from the manufacturer.

C. Disable remote management features on the IoT device to limit network-based attacks.

D. Change the default username and password to a complex, unique credential set.

16) A company engaged a consultant to conduct an offensive security assessment, which includes penetration testing and social engineering. Which of the following teams will conduct this assessment activity?

A. White

B. Purple

C. Blue

D. Red

17) A systems administrator is developing a solution with the following objectives:

Establish a secure zone.

Implement a company-wide access control policy.

Minimize the range of threats.

Which of the following is the systems administrator setting up?

A. Zero Trust

B. AAA

OC. Non-repudiation

D. CIA

18) Which of the following defines the process of concealing code or text within a graphical image?

A. Symmetric encryption

B. Hashing

C. Data masking

D. Steganography

19) What are the most effective methods to guarantee only authorized personnel can access a secure facility? (Choose two).

A. Fencing

B. Video surveillance

C. Badge access

D. Access control vestibule

E. Sign-in sheet

F. Sensor

20) What is the most effective method to prevent and block unknown programs from running?

A. Access control list

B. Application allow list.

C. Host-based firewall

D. DLP solution

21) What steps could a security engineer take to ensure workstations and servers are adequately monitored for unauthorized changes and software?

A. Configure all systems to log scheduled tasks.

B. Collect and monitor all traffic exiting the network.

C. Block traffic based on known malicious signatures.

D. Install endpoint management software on all systems.

22) Which of the following agreement types specifies the timeframe within which a vendor must respond?

A. SOW

B. SLA

C. MOA

D. MOU

23) A security analyst and the management team are evaluating the organizational performance of a recent phishing campaign. The user click-through rate surpassed the acceptable risk threshold, prompting the management team to seek ways to minimize the impact when a user clicks on a link in a phishing message. Which of the following should the analyst do?

A. Place posters around the office to raise awareness of common phishing activities.

B. Implement email security filters to prevent phishing emails from being delivered

C. Update the EDR policies to block automatic execution of downloaded programs.

D. Create additional training for users to recognize the signs of phishing attempts.

24) A software development manager seeks to verify the authenticity of the code produced by the company. Which of the following options is the most appropriate?

A. Testing input validation on the user input fields.

B. Performing code signing on company-developed software.

C. Performing static code analysis on the software.

D. Ensuring secure cookies are use.

25) Which phase of the incident response process involves a security analyst reviewing roles and responsibilities?

A. Preparation

B. Recovery

C. Lessons learned

D. Analysis

26) A systems administrator is modifying the password policy in an enterprise environment and seeks to implement this update across all systems as expeditiously as possible. Which of the following operating system security measures will the administrator most likely use?

A. Deploying PowerShell scripts

B. Pushing GPO update

C. Enabling PAP

D. Updating EDR profiles

27) A security analyst scans a company's public network and identifies a host running a remote desktop service that provides access to the production network. Which of the following changes should the security analyst recommend?

A. Changing the remote desktop port to a non-standard number.

B. Setting up a VPN and placing the jump server inside the firewall.

C. Using a proxy for web connections from the remote desktop server.

D. Connecting the remote server to the domain and increasing the password length.

28) A bank requires all its vendors to implement measures to prevent data loss in the event of a stolen laptop. Which of the following strategies is the bank requiring?

A. Encryption at rest

B. Masking

C. Data classification

D. Permission restrictions

29) An administrator finds that certain files on a database server were recently encrypted. The security logs indicate that the data was last accessed by a domain user. Which of the following best describes the type of attack that occurred?

A. Insider threat

B. Social engineering

C. Watering-hole

D. Unauthorized attacker

30) A security analyst must strengthen network access. One of the requirements is to authenticate users using smart cards. Which of the following should the analyst enable to best meet this requirement?

A. CHAP

B. PEAP

C. MS-CHAPv2

D. EAP-TLS

31) The management team has observed that manually created new accounts do not consistently have accurate access or permissions. Which of the following automation techniques should a systems administrator use to streamline account creation?

A. Guard rail script

B. Ticketing workflow

C. Escalation script

D. User provisioning script

32) What is used to measure the criticality of a vulnerability in a quantitative manner?

A. CVE

B. CVSS

C. CIA

D. CERT

33) An administrator received a notification that a user logged in remotely outside of normal hours and transferred substantial amounts of data to a personal device. Which of the following best describes the user's activity?

A. Penetration testing

B. Phishing campaign

C. External audit

D. Insider threat

34) Which of the following would be most suitable for dynamic environments with frequent changes?

A. RTOS

B. Containers

C. Embedded systems

D. SCADA

35) A company procured cyber insurance to mitigate risks identified in the risk register. Which of the following strategies does this represent?

A. Avoid

B. Mitigate

C. Transfer

D. Accept

36) A systems administrator is seeking a cost-effective, cloud-based application hosting solution. Which of the following meets these requirements?

A. SDN

B. Type 1 hvpervisor

C. Serverless framework

D. SD-WAN

37) A user is trying to apply a patch to a critical system, but the patch fails to transfer. Which of the following access controls is most likely inhibiting the transfer?

A. Attribute-based

B. Time of day

C. Role-based

D. Least privilege

38) An administrator discovers that all user workstations and servers are showing a message related to files with a .ryk extension. Which of the following types of infections is present on the systems?

A. Virus

B. Trojan

C. Spyware

D. Ransomware

39) What is the most effective measure to guard against an employee accidentally installing malware on a company system?

A. Host-based firewall

B. System isolation

C. Least privilege

D. Application allow list

40) What can be utilized to detect potential attacker actions without impacting production servers?

A. Honey pot

B. Video surveillance

C. Zero Trust

D. Geofencing

41) Following a security breach, customers filed a lawsuit against the company. In response, the company's attorneys have requested the security team to implement a legal hold. Which of the following describes the action the security team will most likely be required to take?

A. Retain the emails between the security team and affected customers for 30 days.

B. Retain any communications related to the security breach until further notice.

C. Retain any communications between security members during the breach response.

D. Retain all emails from the company to affected customers for an indefinite period of time.

42) Following an audit, an administrator finds that all users have access to confidential data stored on a file server. Which of the following should the administrator use to restrict access

to the data quickly?

A. Group Policy

B. Content filtering

C. Data loss prevention

D. Access control lists

43) Which two of the following are common vulnerabilities associated with VoIP?

A. SPIM

B. Vishing

C. VLAN hopping

D. Phishing

E. DHCP snooping

F. Tailgating

44) Which of the following practices is most effective in preventing an insider from introducing malicious code into a company's development process?

A. Code scanning for vulnerabilities

B. Open-source component usage

C. Quality assurance testing

D. Peer review and approval

45) Which of the following vulnerabilities is specific to hardware?

A. Firmware version

B. Buffer overflow

C. SQL injection

D. Cross-site scripting

46) What is the best approach to managing a critical business application that is running on a legacy server?

A. Segmentation

B. Isolation

C. Hardening

D. Decommissioning

47) A client requires a service provider's hosted security services to have a minimum uptime of 99.99%. Which of the following documents includes the information the service provider should return to the client?

A. MOA

B. SOW

C. MOU

D. SLA

48) A security analyst is reviewing SIEM alerts concerning potential malicious network traffic originating from an employee's corporate laptop. The analyst has concluded that more information about the executable running on the device is needed to proceed with the investigation. Which of the following logs should the analyst use as a data source?

A. Endpoint

B. Application

C. Network

D. IPS/IDS

49) A security administrator is implementing a DLP solution to stop the exfiltration of sensitive customer data. Which of the following should the administrator do first?

A. Block access to cloud storage websites.

B. Create a rule to block outgoing email attachments.

C. Apply classifications to the data.

D. Remove all user permissions from shares on the file server.

50) An attacker impersonating the Chief Executive Officer calls an employee and instructs them to purchase gift cards. Which of the following techniques is the attacker using?

A. Smishing

B. Disinformation

C. Impersonating

D. Whaling

51) A security practitioner conducts a vulnerability assessment on a company's network and discovers multiple vulnerabilities, which the operations team then resolves. Which of the following should be done next?

A. Initiate a penetration test.

B. Submit a report.

C. Conduct an audit.

D. Rescan the network.

52) An organization has recently updated its security policy to incorporate the following statement:

Regular expressions are utilized in the source code to eliminate special characters like $, I, ;, &, `, and ? from variables set by forms in a web application.

Which of the following best explains the security technique the organization adopted by making this addition to the policy?

A. Input validation

B. Static code analysis

C. Code debugging

D. Identify embedded keys

53) Which of the following choices are suitable for describing

technical security controls? (Select three)

A. Focused on protecting material assets

B. Sometimes called logical security controls

C. Executed by computer systems (instead of people)

D. Also known as administrative controls

E. Implemented with technology

F. Primarily implemented and executed by people (as opposed to computer systems)

54) Which of the options below are examples of technical security controls? (Select three)

A. Security audits

B. Encryption

C. Organizational security policy

D. IDSs

E. Configuration management

F. Firewalls

55) Which of the following choices describe the characteristic features of managerial security controls? (Select three)

A. Also known as administrative controls

B. Sometimes referred to as logical security controls

C. Focused on reducing the risk of security incidents

D. Executed by computer systems (instead of people)

E. Documented in written policies

F. Focused on protecting material assets

56) Which of the following options are examples of managerial security controls? (Select three)

A. Configuration management

B. Data backups

C. Organizational security policy

D. Risk assessments

E. Security awareness training

57) Which of the following options are suitable for describing operational security controls? (Select three)

A. Also known as administrative controls

B. Focused on the day-to-day procedures of an organization

C. Executed by computer systems (instead of people)

D. Used to ensure that the equipment continues to work as specified

E. Focused on managing risk

F. Primarily implemented and executed by people (as opposed to computer systems)

58) Which of the following examples are considered operational security controls? (Select three)

A. Risk assessments

B. Configuration management

C. System backups

D. Authentication protocols

E. Patch management

59) Which of the following options describe security controls that aim to discourage, identify, and stop unauthorized access, theft, damage, or destruction of physical assets?

A. Managerial security controls

B. Physical security controls

C. Technical security controls

D. Operational security controls

60) Which of the following examples are not considered physical security controls? (Select three)

A. Lighting

B. Access control vestibules

C. Data backups

D. Fencing/Bollards/Barricades

E. Firewalls

F. Security guards

G. Asset management

61) Which of the following options are examples of preventive security controls? (Select three)

A. Encryption

B. IDS

C. Sensors

D. Firewalls

E. Warning signs

F. AV software

62) Which of the following are examples of deterrent security controls? (Select three)

A. Warning signs

B. Sensors

C. Lighting

D. Video surveillance

E. Security audits

F. Fencing/Bollards

63) Which of the following options describe detective security controls? (Select all that apply)

A. Lighting

B. Log monitoring

C. Sandboxing

D. Security audits

E. CCTV

F. IDS

G. Vulnerability scanning

64) Which of the following options describe corrective security controls? (Select all that apply)

A. IRPs

B. Log monitoring

C. Backups and system recovery

D. DRPs

E. Forensic analysis

65) Which of the following options describe compensating security controls? (Select all that apply)

A. Temporary service disablement

B. Video surveillance

C. MFA

D. Backup power systems

E. Sandboxing

F. Temporary port blocking

66) "Directive security controls" is a term used to describe

security controls that are implemented through policies and procedures.

A. True

B. False

67) Which of the following terms are examples of directive security controls? (Select two)

A. IRP

B. AUP

C. IDS

D. MFA

E. IPS

68) Which of the following terms describe the fundamental principles of information security?

A. PKI

B. AAA

C. GDPR

D. CIA

69) Non-repudiation refers to the inability to deny responsibility for an action. In data security, it ensures confidentiality, integrity, and origin of data.

A. True

B. False

70) Which of the following most accurately describes the concept of non-repudiation?

A. Digital certificate

B. MFA

C. Hashing

D. Encryption

71) Which type of user account contradicts the principle of non-repudiation?

A. Standard user account

B. Shared account

C. Guest user account

D. Service account

72) Which aspect of the AAA security architecture handles confirming the identity of an individual or process?

A. Authentication

B. Authorization

C. Accounting

73) In the AAA security architecture, the process of allowing or denying access to resources is called:

A. Authentication

B. Authorization

C. Accounting

74) In the AAA security architecture, the process of monitoring accessed services and the quantity of resources used is referred to as:

A. Authentication

B. Authorization

C. Accounting

75) Which of the following solutions offer(s) AAA functionality? (Select all that apply)

A. CHAP

B. TACACS+

C. PAP

D. RADIUS

E. MS-CHAP

76) In the context of the AAA framework, typical methods for authenticating individuals include: (Select three)

A. IP addresses

B. Usernames and passwords

C. MAC addresses

D. Biometrics

E. MFA

77) Which of the following options describe common methods of device authentication used in the AAA framework? (Select three)

A. Usernames and passwords

B. Digital certificates

C. IP addresses

D. MFA

E. Biometric authentication

F. MAC addresses

78) A company is preparing to launch a security awareness campaign centered on recognizing email-based threats. Which option would be the BEST to include in the campaign to effectively educate employees on recognizing and reporting potential phishing attempts?

A. Hosting a quarterly security seminar that covers a range of security awareness topics, including phishing.

B. Sending out a company-wide email with a list of tips for identifying phishing emails.

C. Conducting tailored phishing exercises with immediate feedback for employees who fall for the simulated attack.

D. Distributing a monthly newsletter that covers various topics, including a brief section on email security.

79) In a Zero Trust security model, resources are accessible to everyone by default and Access is restricted based on user behavior or other analytics in a Zero Trust security model.

A. True

B. False

80) When securing an environment that utilizes a real-time operating system, what primary characteristic of this system type must be considered?

A. Wide range of application compatibility

B. Predictable timing and performance

C. Focus on user interface design

D. Multi-user support

81) What is likely to be directly affected when a company does not comply with data protection regulations and this non-compliance becomes public knowledge?

A. Reputational damage

B. Service-Level Agreement renegotiation

C. Annualized Loss Expectancy

D. Data ownership transfer

82) The company's security team has upgraded the network firewall to a newer model to improve security features. As a security analyst, what is the most critical action to take after the upgrade to ensure continued operational efficiency?

A. Perform a complete network penetration test to identify potential new vulnerabilities introduced.

B. Schedule a meeting with the stakeholders to discuss the possibility of future upgrades.

C. Implement additional firewall rules to immediately increase the security posture without a scheduled review.

D. Update the security policies and network configuration documentation to reflect changes made by the new firewall.

83) Which authorization model utilizes specific protocols created to transfer a user's authentication and authorization information across distinct security domains?

A. Mandatory Access Control (MAC)

B. Role-Based Access Control (RBAC)

C. Discretionary Access Control (DAC)

D. Federated identity management

84) Your employer has decided to transition part of their operations to the cloud. The objective of this move is to eliminate the need for maintaining onsite data centers to run their software. Which cloud model would the company want

to utilize?

A. IaaS

B. PaaS

C. XaaS

D. SaaS

85) An organization has assembled key personnel to discuss disaster recovery plans and individual responsibilities through scenario-based discussions. This is an example of which type of testing?

A. Simulation

B. Tabletop exercises

C. Parallel processing

D. Fail over

86) Your organization recently suffered an attack, and you need to analyze the incident to determine how it occurred and how to prevent similar future incidents. Which type of control would be best suited for this purpose?

A. Preventive controls

B. Detective controls

C. Compensating controls

D. Corrective controls

87) A security analyst observes an unusual increase in administrator-level account logins to a sensitive system outside of the scheduled maintenance windows. While investigating the logs for this out-of-cycle event, which of the following would BEST indicate potential unauthorized access?

A. Resource consumption

B. Impossible travel

C. None of these

D. Concurrent session usage

88) Your employer has historically prioritized security and has not utilized any company-owned mobile or wireless devices, such as laptops and smartphones.

A new project has been initiated to assess market options for securely implementing laptops within the company.

One stipulation is that all data stored on the laptop's drive must be encrypted.

What type of drive could fulfill this requirement?

A. PKI-SSD

B. VPN

C. RAID 0

D. SED

89) An IT security team has deployed decoy files within the organization's network to deceive and trap potential attackers.

These resources appear functional and contain seemingly valuable data but are closely monitored for interactions to detect malicious activity.

Which of the following best describes these fake resources?

A. Honeypot

B. DNS Sinkhole

C. Honeynet

D. Intrusion Detection System (IDS)

E. Honeytoken

F. Firewall

90) Your company is partnering with a vendor to implement a new customer relationship management system.

To safeguard your proprietary data and client information during discussions, what should be signed before sharing detailed system specifications and data flows?

A. Memorandum of Understanding (MOU)

B. Non-Disclosure Agreement (NDA)

C. Master Service Agreement (MSA)

D. Service-Level Agreement (SLA)

ANSWERS AND EXPLANATION

1) The most likely solution to allow users to access the new retail website while maintaining security is:

D. Updating the categorization in the content filter

Here's why the other options wouldn't be ideal solutions:

A. Creating a firewall rule to allow HTTPS traffic: While HTTPS encrypts website traffic, it wouldn't necessarily address the website's classification as gambling content if that's the reason for blocking.

B. Configuring the IPS to allow shopping: An IPS (Intrusion Prevention System) focuses on blocking malicious activity, not website categories. Configuring it to allow "shopping" wouldn't be a targeted approach.

C. Tuning the DLP rule that detects credit card data: DLP (Data Loss Prevention) typically focuses on preventing sensitive data from leaving the organization, not website access. While the website might involve online shopping, adjusting the DLP rule wouldn't directly address the content filtering issue.

By updating the categorization in the content filter, the organization can reclassify the website from "gambling" to a more appropriate category (e.g., "retail"). This would allow legitimate access to the site while maintaining security measures for other content categories.

Here are some additional points to consider:

Reviewing the website: It's advisable to ensure the website is indeed a legitimate retail store before updating the filter category.

User education: Educating users about responsible online shopping practices can be a valuable security measure.

2) Out of the listed options, the most important reason for conducting root cause analysis in incident response is:

D. To prevent future incidents of the same nature.

Here's why:

LoCs (Lines of Code): While understanding the affected code might be relevant in some cases, a root cause analysis focuses on broader system or network issues, not necessarily specific lines of code.

Identifying affected systems: This is an important initial step in incident response, but it's not the ultimate goal of a root cause analysis.

Eradicating malware: This is crucial during incident response, but it's a separate step from the root cause analysis, which focuses on identifying the underlying reasons why the incident occurred.

Root cause analysis delves deeper than just identifying the immediate cause of an incident. It aims to understand the root factors that contributed to the event, such as vulnerabilities in systems, misconfigurations, or security policy gaps. By uncovering these root causes, organizations can implement corrective actions to prevent similar incidents from happening again in the future.

Here are some benefits of performing a thorough root cause analysis:

Improved security posture: By addressing the underlying causes of incidents, organizations can strengthen their overall security posture and reduce the risk of future attacks.

More effective remediation: Understanding the root cause helps in implementing targeted remediation efforts to prevent similar incidents, rather than just patching the immediate symptoms.

Informed decision-making: Insights from the root cause analysis can inform security investments and resource allocation to address the most critical vulnerabilities.

Therefore, root cause analysis plays a vital role in incident response by helping organizations learn from security breaches and proactively prevent future occurrences.

3) Out of the options provided, the most suitable answer for verifying a certificate when presented to a user is:

A. OCSP (Online Certificate Status Protocol)

Here's why:

OCSP: This protocol allows a client to check the revocation status of a certificate with a trusted Certificate Authority (CA) in real-time. When a user encounters a website's certificate, the user's browser can leverage OCSP to verify if the certificate has been revoked by the issuing CA, potentially indicating a security compromise.

CSR (Certificate Signing Request): This is a message sent by an entity to a CA requesting a digital certificate. It wouldn't be used for verification after the certificate is issued.

CA (Certificate Authority): A CA is a trusted entity that issues and signs digital certificates. While CAs play a crucial role in the certificate lifecycle, they wouldn't directly verify the certificate presented to a user.

CRC (Cyclic Redundancy Check): This is a checksum used to detect data errors during transmission. While CRCs can be used for data integrity checks, they wouldn't specifically verify the validity of a digital certificate.

Therefore, OCSP offers a real-time mechanism for users (through their browsers) to verify the validity of a presented certificate with the issuing CA, ensuring its authenticity and preventing potential man-in-the-middle attacks.

4) Out of the listed options, the most suitable solution for quickly mitigating a network access vulnerability in legacy IoT devices is:

C. Segmentation

Here's why segmentation is the best choice for a quick response:

Insurance: While insurance might help offset financial losses from a security incident, it wouldn't directly address the technical vulnerability itself.

Patching: Patching would be the ideal solution in the long run, but it might not be readily available for legacy devices, especially if they are no longer supported by the manufacturer. Patching could also take time to deploy across all affected devices.

Segmentation: This involves isolating the vulnerable IoT devices on a separate network segment from critical systems. This can be implemented relatively quickly and limits the potential blast radius of an exploit targeting the vulnerability. Even if an attacker gains access to a vulnerable device, segmentation can prevent them from pivoting to other parts of the network.

Replacement: Replacing all legacy devices would be the most secure option in the long term, but it's often the most expensive and time-consuming solution. It might not be feasible for a quick response.

While segmentation isn't a perfect solution, it offers a fast and effective way to mitigate the immediate risk associated with the vulnerability until a more permanent solution (like patching) can be implemented.

Here are some additional considerations:

Restricting network access: Further controls can be implemented within the segmented network to restrict the vulnerable devices' ability to communicate with unauthorized systems or the internet.

Monitoring network traffic: Monitoring the segmented network for suspicious activity can help detect potential exploitation attempts.

By implementing segmentation quickly, the organization can significantly reduce the risk of attackers leveraging the vulnerability in the legacy IoT devices to gain access to critical systems.

5) Out of the listed options, the incident response activity that describes the process of determining the origin of an incident is:

A. Analysis

Here's why the other options wouldn't be the most suitable answers for this scenario:

Lessons learned: This phase typically occurs after the incident has been contained and eradicated. It focuses on identifying takeaways and improvements for future responses.

Detection: This refers to the initial identification of a security incident. While it might provide clues about the origin, a deeper analysis is required to pinpoint the source.

Containment: This phase concentrates on stopping the ongoing attack and preventing further damage. While containment can provide some context about the nature of the incident, it might not necessarily reveal the exact origin.

Analysis involves a thorough examination of collected evidence, including log files, network traffic data, and affected systems. This analysis helps the incident response team to reconstruct the attacker's actions and identify the initial point of entry or compromise.

Here are some specific activities involved in the analysis phase:

Log analysis: Examining system logs, firewall logs, and other relevant sources for suspicious activity.

Network traffic analysis: Investigating network traffic patterns to identify potential points of intrusion.

Malware analysis: Analyzing any discovered malware to understand its capabilities and potential origin.

Timeline creation: Constructing a timeline of events to map the attacker's movements within the system.

By performing a comprehensive analysis, the incident response team can gain valuable insights into the origin of the incident, which can be crucial for implementing targeted remediation efforts and preventing similar attacks in the future.

6) Answer: B. Confidential, F. Restricted.

Explanation:

Confidential: The project information is likely to be classified as confidential due to its sensitive nature and the need to protect it from unauthorized access.

Restricted: Given the critical nature of the system and the government's involvement, the data is likely to be restricted to authorized personnel only to ensure its security and integrity.

Data classification involves assigning labels to data based on its sensitivity and business impact. Various organizations and sectors may employ different classification schemes, but a common one includes:

Public: Data that can be freely shared with no harm or risk.

Private: Data for internal use only, with potential harm if disclosed.

Confidential: Data for authorized use only, with significant harm if disclosed.

Restricted: Data for extremely limited use, with severe harm if disclosed.

In this scenario, the company is developing a critical system for the government and storing project information on a file share. This data is likely to be classified as confidential and restricted due to its sensitive nature, potential for harm if disclosed, and the need to protect national security or public safety. The government may also impose specific requirements for handling such data, including encryption, access control, and auditing.

7) Out of the listed options, the most likely outcome for a large bank failing an internal PCI DSS compliance assessment is:

C. Fines

Here's why:

Audit findings: The internal assessment itself would identify the audit findings, highlighting areas where the bank is non-compliant with PCI DSS standards.

Sanctions: Sanctions are broader than fines and could encompass a wider range of penalties. While some regulatory bodies might impose sanctions for non-compliance, fines are a more direct and likely consequence identified during an internal assessment.

Fines: PCI DSS non-compliance can lead to significant financial penalties from payment card brands (e.g., Visa, Mastercard) depending on the severity of the violations and the number of card transactions processed. For a large bank, these fines can be substantial.

Reputation damage: While failing a PCI DSS assessment can certainly damage a bank's reputation, it wouldn't be the most immediate outcome identified during an internal assessment. The internal assessment would focus on identifying and rectifying compliance gaps to avoid future consequences like fines and reputational damage.

Therefore, fines are the most likely outcome for a large bank failing an internal PCI DSS compliance assessment, as they are a direct financial penalty imposed by payment card brands for non-compliance.

It's important to note that failing an internal assessment serves as a warning sign. By addressing the identified gaps and achieving compliance, the bank can avoid the potential for fines and reputational damage in the future.

8) Out of the listed options, the optimal method for consistently checking daily whether security settings on servers have been altered is:

D. Automation

Here's why automation is the best choice for daily security setting checks:

Scalability: Manually checking numerous servers every day would be time-consuming and error-prone. Automation allows for consistent checks across a large number of servers efficiently.

Frequency: Automating the process ensures daily checks occur without fail, unlike manual audits which might be scheduled less frequently.

Accuracy: Automation reduces the possibility of human error that can occur during manual security setting reviews.

Let's see why the other options wouldn't be ideal solutions:

Manual audit: While manual audits can be valuable for in-depth security assessments, they wouldn't be suitable for daily checks due to the reasons mentioned above.

Attestation: Attestation involves a formal statement confirming adherence to a security policy. While it can be a complementary control, it wouldn't provide the ongoing monitoring of security settings that automation offers.

Compliance checklist: A checklist can be a helpful tool for security audits, but it wouldn't be automated and wouldn't provide the continuous monitoring required for daily checks.

Automated tools can be configured to:

Compare current server configurations against a baseline: This baseline represents the desired secure state of the server settings.

Alert administrators: If any discrepancies are detected, automated notifications can be sent to IT security personnel for further investigation and remediation.

By automating daily security setting checks, organizations can proactively identify and address configuration changes that might introduce security vulnerabilities.

9) Out of the listed options, the most suitable description for the scenario is:

B. Network segmentation

Here's why:

Network segmentation: This involves dividing a network into smaller segments to limit the blast radius of a security incident. In this case, the host-based firewall on the legacy Linux system acts as a control point, restricting access only to authorized internal IP addresses. This helps to isolate the system and minimize the potential impact if it were compromised.

Let's explore why the other options aren't the best fit:

Compensating control: While the firewall could be considered a compensating control in a broader sense (addressing potential vulnerabilities in the legacy system), the primary focus here is on network segmentation achieved through the firewall's access control rules.

Transfer of risk: This refers to shifting the financial responsibility for a risk to another party (e.g., insurance). Permitting connections only from specific internal IPs doesn't involve transferring risk, it focuses on controlling network access.

SNMP traps: These are alerts generated by network devices. While the firewall might utilize SNMP for monitoring purposes, it wouldn't be directly related to the access control functionality described in the scenario.

By allowing connections only from specific internal IP addresses, the firewall essentially creates a network segment around the legacy Linux system. This segmentation helps to improve the overall security posture by limiting the attack surface and potential lateral movement within the network if the system were compromised.

10) Out of the listed options, the most suitable method for a security administrator to identify certificates requiring updates is:

D. CRL (Certificate Revocation List)

Here's why CRL is the best choice:

CRL (Certificate Revocation List): This is a list published by a certificate authority (CA) containing certificates that have been revoked before their expiration date. By comparing the certificates installed on the company's machines with the CRL, the administrator can determine if any certificates have been invalidated by the CA and need to be replaced.

SCEP (Simple Certificate Enrollment Protocol): This protocol is used to automate the process of requesting and enrolling certificates from a CA. It wouldn't directly tell you if existing certificates are revoked.

OCSP (Online Certificate Status Protocol): While OCSP also checks the revocation status of certificates, it requires individual queries for each certificate. For a bulk check of certificates on multiple machines, a CRL is a more efficient approach.

CSR (Certificate Signing Request): This is a message sent by an entity to a CA requesting a new certificate. It wouldn't be used to check the status of existing certificates.

Here's how a security administrator can leverage CRLs:

Obtain the CRL: Download the CRL from the certificate vendor's website.

Distribute the CRL: Distribute the CRL to the relevant systems or use a mechanism like CRL caching to ensure local availability.

Certificate verification: Use software tools or system settings to verify the installed certificates against the downloaded CRL. This process will identify any certificates that have been revoked and need to be updated.

By utilizing CRLs, the security administrator can efficiently identify revoked certificates and ensure that company machines are using valid certificates for secure communication.

11) Out of the listed options, the most appropriate next step for the security manager after developing new security incident response (IR) documents is:

D. Conduct a tabletop exercise with the team.

Here's why:

Tabletop exercise: This is a simulated security incident scenario where the IR team can walk through the newly created documentation, test their understanding of the procedures, and identify any potential gaps or areas for improvement. This helps ensure the effectiveness of the IR plan and allows the team to practice their response under controlled conditions.

Let's see why the other options wouldn't be the most immediate next step:

A. Maximum data retention policy: While data retention policies are important, setting the maximum specifically at this stage isn't necessarily the most crucial next action. The focus should be on testing and refining the IR procedures first.

B. Secure storage: Secure storage of the IR documents is important, but it can be addressed after validating the procedures themselves.

C. Data classification: While data classification of the IR documents is relevant for information security, it's less critical than testing the procedures through a tabletop exercise.

A tabletop exercise allows the security manager to:

Identify potential issues: Simulating real-world scenarios can reveal ambiguities or missing steps in the documentation.

Improve communication: The exercise fosters communication and collaboration among team members, ensuring everyone understands their roles and responsibilities during an incident.

Test response capabilities: This exercise provides a safe environment to test the team's ability to follow the documented procedures and use relevant tools for incident response.

By conducting a tabletop exercise, the security manager can solidify the newly developed IR documents and ensure the team is prepared to effectively respond to different security incidents.

12) Out of the listed options, the authentication framework that supports multiple authentication methods for wireless networks and Point-to-Point connections is:

C. Extensible Authentication Protocol (EAP)

Here's why EAP is the answer:

Core Functionality: EAP is a framework, not a specific authentication method itself. It defines a standard way for different authentication methods (called EAP methods) to be negotiated and used between a client and a server during network access.

Multiple Method Support: EAP supports a wide range of authentication methods, including PEAP (Protected EAP), TLS (Transport Layer Security), TTLS (Tunneled TLS), and more. This allows for flexibility in choosing the most appropriate authentication method based on security requirements.

Let's explore why the other options are not correct:

A. Simple Network Management Protocol (SNMP): SNMP is a protocol for managing network devices, not for user authentication.

B. Protected Extensible Authentication Protocol (PEAP): PEAP is one specific EAP method that uses a tunneled TLS connection to provide secure authentication. While it leverages EAP, it's not the framework itself.

D. Lightweight Extensible Authentication Protocol (LEAP): LEAP is a proprietary EAP method developed by Cisco. It's not as secure as other methods like PEAP or EAP-TLS and is not widely recommended due to security vulnerabilities.

Extensible Authentication Protocol (EAP) is an authentication framework commonly used in network and internet connections. It supports diverse authentication methods, including token cards, smart cards, certificates, and one-time passwords. EAP is widely implemented in wireless network standards like WPA and WPA2, providing flexible authentication mechanisms that can adapt based on the required security policies.

13) Out of the listed options, the most suitable solution for detecting rootkits in the future is:

C. EDR (Endpoint Detection and Response)

Here's why EDR is the best choice:

EDR (Endpoint Detection and Response): This is a security solution that goes beyond traditional antivirus by continuously monitoring endpoint activity for suspicious behaviors. EDR can be effective in detecting rootkits because they often exhibit unusual behaviors like hidden processes, file system modifications, or network communication patterns.

Let's explore why the other options wouldn't be ideal for rootkit detection:

FDE (Full Disk Encryption): While FDE encrypts the entire disk, it wouldn't necessarily detect the presence of a rootkit. It's a preventative measure that can protect data even if a rootkit is installed, but it wouldn't actively identify the rootkit itself.

NIDS (Network Intrusion Detection System): NIDS primarily focuses on monitoring network traffic for malicious activity. While some rootkit network activity might be detected, NIDS wouldn't necessarily have visibility into the specific behaviors of a rootkit operating on individual endpoints (PCs) within the subnet.

DLP (Data Loss Prevention): DLP is designed to prevent sensitive data exfiltration, but it wouldn't be directly focused on detecting rootkits themselves.

EDR offers advanced capabilities like:

Endpoint behavior monitoring: EDR monitors processes, file system activity, and registry changes on endpoints, which can help identify deviations from normal behavior indicative of a rootkit.

Anomaly detection: EDR can analyze endpoint activity and identify anomalies that might suggest the presence of a rootkit, even if it hasn't been previously identified.

Threat hunting: EDR can be used for proactive threat hunting, allowing security teams to search for specific indicators of compromise (IOCs) associated with known rootkits.

By implementing EDR, organizations can gain deeper visibility into endpoint activity and improve their ability to detect and respond to threats like rootkits effectively. This can help prevent future outbreaks and ensure successful remediation efforts.

14) Out of the listed options, the attack surface a Network Access Control (NAC) platform is designed to protect is:

B. Wired network connections

Here's why NAC focuses on wired connections:

NAC functionality: NAC enforces access control policies on network devices by authenticating and authorizing them before granting access to the network. This primarily applies to wired network connections where devices connect using ethernet cables.

Let's see why the other options wouldn't be the primary targets for NAC:

A. Bluetooth: While NAC might be able to identify Bluetooth

devices in some cases, it wouldn't be the main focus of NAC controls. Bluetooth connections are typically managed through separate security configurations.

C. NFC (Near Field Communication): Similar to Bluetooth, NAC wouldn't be directly involved in controlling NFC connections, which have a shorter range and different use cases.

D. SCADA (Supervisory Control and Data Acquisition): SCADA systems are often part of industrial control systems (ICS) and might have specific security requirements beyond the scope of traditional NAC solutions.

Here's how NAC helps secure wired network connections:

Device authentication: NAC can authenticate devices connecting to the network, ensuring they are authorized devices and not imposters.

Device posture checks: NAC can enforce security policies on devices, such as requiring them to have up-to-date antivirus software or specific security configurations, before granting access.

Network segmentation: NAC can be used to segment the network, restricting access of certain devices to specific areas of the network based on their role or security posture.

By implementing NAC, the systems administrator aims to improve the security of the wired network by controlling device access and enforcing security policies. This can help prevent unauthorized devices from gaining access to the network and potentially contributing to security incidents.

15) Out of the listed options, the BEST immediate step to mitigate the risk of a compromised IoT device with default credentials is:

D. Change the default username and password to a complex, unique credential set.

Here's why changing credentials is the most critical initial action:

High Risk of Exploitation: Default credentials are well-known to attackers and can be easily exploited using automated tools. This makes the device highly vulnerable to unauthorized access and potential takeover.

Immediate Mitigation: Changing the credentials immediately addresses the most critical vulnerability, significantly reducing the attack surface.

Let's explore why the other options, while important, come after the initial mitigation step:

A. Vulnerability Scan: While a vulnerability scan can be valuable to identify other weaknesses in the device, it's not the most urgent action. The device is already vulnerable due to the default credentials.

B. Firmware Update: Updating the firmware might address security vulnerabilities, but it's not guaranteed, and it shouldn't be done before changing the default credentials to prevent unauthorized access during the update process.

C. Disabling Remote Management: While disabling remote management features can limit attack vectors, it might also hinder legitimate management of the device. It's a consideration after securing the device with a strong password.

Therefore, changing the default credentials is the most crucial and immediate step to mitigate the risk posed by the vulnerable IoT device. Once this is done, the other security measures can be addressed.

16) Out of the listed options, the team that would conduct an offensive security assessment, including penetration testing and social engineering, is:

D. Red Team

Here's why:

Red Team: Red teams are also known as ethical hackers. They simulate real-world attacker behavior to identify vulnerabilities in an organization's security posture. Penetration testing and social engineering are common tactics used by red teams to exploit these vulnerabilities.

White Team: White teams are the internal security team within an organization. They are responsible for protecting the organization's assets and may work alongside red teams during an offensive security assessment.

Purple Team: Purple teams are a combination of red and blue teams. They work together to continuously improve the organization's security posture by simulating attacks and identifying potential weaknesses.

Blue Team: Blue teams are the internal security team responsible for defending the organization's network and systems from cyberattacks. While they might collaborate with red teams during an assessment, they wouldn't be the ones conducting the offensive activities themselves.

Therefore, the consultant has likely engaged a red team to conduct the offensive security assessment, leveraging penetration testing and social engineering techniques to evaluate the organization's security controls and identify potential security risks.

17) Out of the listed options, the concept the systems administrator is setting up is most likely:

A. Zero Trust

Here's why Zero Trust best aligns with the administrator's objectives:

Secure zone: Zero Trust doesn't rely solely on perimeter security but creates a secure zone by implementing access controls throughout the network.

Company-wide access control policy: Zero Trust enforces a strict access control policy where all users and devices must be continuously authenticated and authorized before granting access to resources, regardless of location.

Minimize the range of threats: By minimizing trust and requiring constant verification, Zero Trust helps reduce the potential impact of a security breach by limiting lateral movement within the network.

Let's explore why the other options wouldn't be the most suitable fit:

AAA (Authentication, Authorization, and Accounting): While AAA is a foundational security concept used in access control, it doesn't encompass the broader security posture envisioned in Zero Trust. AAA focuses on the technical aspects of user verification and access control, whereas Zero Trust incorporates a "never trust, always verify" approach throughout the entire security strategy.

Non-repudiation: This security principle ensures that a transaction cannot be denied by any party involved. While Zero Trust can strengthen non-repudiation by improving access control logging, it's not the primary objective in this scenario.

CIA (Confidentiality, Integrity, Availability): This is a security triad outlining essential security goals, but it doesn't represent a specific security architecture like Zero Trust. Zero Trust can support achieving CIA by establishing secure access controls that protect confidentiality, integrity, and availability of data and systems.

Therefore, considering the focus on creating a secure zone, enforcing company-wide access control, and minimizing threats, Zero Trust best reflects the systems administrator's goals. Zero Trust goes beyond traditional perimeter-based security and aims to continuously verify trust before granting access throughout the network.

18) Out of the listed options, the process of concealing code or text within a graphical image is defined by:

D. Steganography

Here's why:

Steganography: This technique involves hiding information within another medium, such as hiding code or text within a seemingly innocuous image file. The hidden information is typically undetectable to the human eye.

Let's explore why the other options wouldn't be suitable for this scenario:

Symmetric encryption: This is a type of encryption where the same secret key is used for both encryption and decryption. While encryption can be used to hide the contents of a file, it wouldn't necessarily conceal the data within another file format like an image.

Hashing: This is a one-way cryptographic function that transforms data into a unique fixed-size value (hash). Hashing doesn't conceal data but rather creates a fingerprint of the data for verification purposes.

Data masking: This involves replacing sensitive data with fictitious characters, often used to protect data privacy during testing or development. While it hides the actual data, it wouldn't involve embedding it within another file format.

Steganography can be used for legitimate purposes, such as embedding copyright information in images. However, it can also be misused to hide malicious code or sensitive information within seemingly harmless files.

19) Here are the two most effective methods to guarantee only authorized personnel can access a secure facility:

C. Badge access: This system utilizes electronic badges or keycards that are programmed to grant access only to authorized individuals. When presented at a reader, the badge verifies the user's identity and grants access if they are authorized to enter the secure facility.

D. Access control vestibule: Also known as a mantrap or security vestibule, this is a physical security measure that creates a double-doored entryway. Personnel must gain access through the first door using their credentials (e.g., badge), and the second door won't unlock until the first door is securely closed. This prevents unauthorized individuals from tailgating someone who has gained legitimate access.

Let's explore why the other options might be helpful but aren't the most effective choices on their own:

A. Fencing: While fencing can create a physical barrier, it doesn't inherently control who can access the facility. It can be a deterrent, but it should be used in conjunction with other access control methods.

B. Video surveillance: This can be a valuable tool for monitoring activity and potentially identifying unauthorized access after the fact. However, it wouldn't necessarily prevent unauthorized access in real-time.

E. Sign-in sheet: Sign-in sheets can provide a record of who entered the facility, but they are not a secure access control method. Someone with malicious intent could easily forge a signature.

F. Sensor: Sensors can be used for various purposes, such as detecting motion or unauthorized entry attempts. However, they need to be integrated into a broader access control system to be truly effective. For example, a sensor might detect unauthorized entry, but it wouldn't necessarily prevent it without additional measures like alarms or automatic door locks.

Therefore, by combining badge access with an access control vestibule, organizations can significantly enhance the security of a facility and ensure only authorized personnel can gain entry. These methods provide robust access control mechanisms that require valid credentials and prevent unauthorized individuals from following someone with authorized access.

20) Out of the listed options, the most effective method to prevent and block unknown programs from running is:

B. Application allow list (also known as application whitelisting)

Here's why application allowlisting is the best choice:

Application allow list: This approach creates a list of authorized applications that are explicitly permitted to run on the system. Any program not on the list is automatically blocked, preventing unknown or unauthorized programs from executing. This offers a strong preventive measure against unknown threats.

Access control list (ACL): ACLs can be used to control access to resources like files or network ports. While they can be helpful in certain scenarios, they wouldn't necessarily prevent all unknown programs from running. An unknown program might still be able to execute if it has access to the resources it needs.

Host-based firewall: Firewalls primarily focus on controlling network traffic and might not be able to comprehensively block unknown programs from running within the system itself.

DLP solution: Data Loss Prevention (DLP) solutions are designed to prevent sensitive data exfiltration. While they might be able to identify and block programs attempting to transmit data, they wouldn't necessarily block all unknown programs from execution.

Application allowlisting offers a proactive approach to prevent unknown programs from running. By only allowing authorized applications, organizations can significantly reduce the risk of malware or unauthorized code execution on their systems. However, it's important to note that maintaining an allowlist requires ongoing effort to ensure authorized applications are included and the list is updated as needed.

21) Out of the listed options, the most suitable step a security engineer can take to monitor workstations and servers for unauthorized changes and software installations is:

D. Install endpoint management software on all systems.

Here's why endpoint management software is the best choice:

Endpoint management software: This software provides centralized visibility and control over endpoints (workstations and servers). It can be configured to:

Track software installations and changes.

Identify unauthorized applications.

Monitor for suspicious activity that might indicate unauthorized modifications.

Let's see why the other options wouldn't be the most effective for this specific purpose:

A. Configure all systems to log scheduled tasks: While logging scheduled tasks can be helpful for auditing purposes, it wouldn't necessarily identify unauthorized changes or software installations. Scheduled tasks could be legitimate.

B. Collect and monitor all traffic exiting the network: This approach (often used by network traffic analysis (NTA) tools) can be valuable for detecting malicious activity, but it wouldn't directly monitor changes on individual workstations or servers.

C. Block traffic based on known malicious signatures: This is a reactive approach using signature-based intrusion detection/ prevention systems (IDS/IPS). While it can help block known threats, it wouldn't necessarily identify unauthorized software installations on endpoints.

Endpoint management software offers a proactive approach for monitoring endpoint activity, including software installations and changes. This allows security engineers to identify potential security risks and take timely action to prevent unauthorized modifications.

Here are some additional functionalities of endpoint management software that can be leveraged for this purpose:

File integrity monitoring: This can detect unauthorized modifications to critical system files.

Software inventory: This provides a comprehensive list of installed software on endpoints, allowing for easy identification of unauthorized applications.

Vulnerability scanning: This can identify vulnerabilities in installed software that could be exploited by attackers.

By implementing endpoint management software and utilizing its monitoring capabilities, security engineers can gain better visibility into endpoint activity and proactively address unauthorized changes and software installations, improving the overall security posture of the organization.

22) Out of the listed options, the agreement type that specifies the timeframe within which a vendor must respond is:

B. SLA (Service Level Agreement)

Here's why an SLA is the most relevant choice:

SLA (Service Level Agreement): This agreement explicitly defines the service levels expected from a vendor, including metrics for performance, availability, and response times. An SLA will typically outline the timeframe within which the vendor must acknowledge and respond to service disruptions or other issues.

Let's explore why the other options wouldn't necessarily specify response timeframes:

A. SOW (Statement of Work): An SOW outlines the specific tasks or deliverables associated with a project and the associated costs. While it might mention deadlines for project completion, it wouldn't necessarily focus on ongoing response times for support or service issues.

C. MOA (Memorandum of Agreement): An MOA is a less formal agreement outlining the high-level understanding between parties regarding a collaboration or project. It wouldn't typically delve into specific service levels or response times.

D. MOU (Memorandum of Understanding): Similar to an MOA, an MOU is a non-binding agreement that outlines a general understanding between parties. It wouldn't necessarily specify technical details like response timeframes.

An SLA goes beyond simply defining services; it establishes measurable expectations for performance and response times. This ensures the vendor is held accountable for meeting specific service levels, including how quickly they must address problems.

Here are some additional details often included in an SLA:

Escalation procedures: The SLA will outline the process for escalating issues if the vendor doesn't meet the agreed-upon response times.

Service credits: Some SLAs include provisions for service credits to be issued to the customer if the vendor fails to meet specific performance metrics.

By having a well-defined SLA in place, organizations can ensure they receive the level of service they expect from their vendors, including timely responses to issues.

23) Out of the listed options, the most suitable action for the security analyst to address the high click-through rate in a phishing campaign is:

D. Create additional training for users to recognize the signs of phishing attempts.

Here's why additional user training is the best choice:

Phishing awareness training: While other options can be complementary, user training is crucial in this scenario. The high click-through rate indicates users might not be adequately equipped to identify phishing attempts. Additional training can help them recognize common phishing tactics, suspicious email elements (e.g., sender address, urgency, grammar), and best practices for handling suspicious emails (e.g., not clicking links, reporting emails).

Let's see why the other options wouldn't be the sole solution in this case:

A. Posters: While raising awareness is helpful, posters alone might not be enough to significantly improve click-through rates. Users need more in-depth training to understand the nuances of phishing attempts.

B. Email security filters: Email filters can be helpful in blocking some phishing emails, but they are not foolproof. Phishing emails are constantly evolving, and attackers can develop techniques to bypass filters. User training can provide a crucial last line of defense.

C. EDR policy update: Updating Endpoint Detection and Response (EDR) policies to block automatic execution can help prevent malware infection if a user clicks a malicious link. However, it wouldn't necessarily address the root cause of the problem, which is users falling victim to phishing attempts in the first place.

By prioritizing user training on recognizing phishing attempts, the security analyst can equip users with the knowledge and skills to make better decisions when encountering suspicious emails. This can significantly reduce the risk of users clicking on malicious links and potentially compromising sensitive information or systems.

Here are some additional training considerations:

Interactive training: Interactive training sessions can be more engaging and effective than simply presenting information.

Simulated phishing attacks: Simulations can provide users with a realistic experience in identifying phishing attempts.

Regular training refreshers: Regularly reinforcing phishing awareness through training refreshers can help users stay vigilant.

By implementing a comprehensive user training program alongside other security measures, the organization can significantly reduce the risk of successful phishing attacks and improve its overall cybersecurity posture.

24) Out of the listed options, the most appropriate method for a software development manager to verify the code's authenticity produced by the company is:

B. Performing code signing on company-developed software

Here's why code signing is the best choice for authenticity verification:

Code signing: This process involves applying a digital signature to the software code. The signature is created using a cryptographic key unique to the company. When the software is executed, the signature can be verified to ensure the code hasn't been tampered with since it was signed. This helps to confirm that the code originates from the trusted source (the company) and hasn't been modified by unauthorized individuals.

Let's explore why the other options address different aspects of software security but wouldn't directly verify code authenticity:

A. Testing input validation on the user input fields: This is an important security practice to prevent vulnerabilities like injection attacks. However, it doesn't directly verify the authenticity of the code itself.

C. Performing static code analysis on the software: This technique can identify potential security vulnerabilities, coding errors, and other issues within the code. While it can improve code quality and security, it wouldn't necessarily confirm the code's origin.

D. Ensuring secure cookies are used: Secure cookies are an important security measure for web applications, but they wouldn't be directly applicable to verifying the authenticity of the entire software codebase.

Code signing establishes a trust chain. When the code is signed with the company's private key, and the signature is successfully validated, it assures users that the code is authentic and hasn't been tampered with since it was signed by the trusted source. This can be particularly important for software distributed to external users or deployed in critical systems.

25) Out of the listed phases of the incident response process, the one that involves a security analyst reviewing roles and responsibilities is:

A. Preparation

Here's why the preparation phase is the most relevant:

Preparation phase: This is the foundational stage of incident response. It focuses on establishing processes, procedures, and resources to effectively handle security incidents. Reviewing roles and responsibilities is a crucial aspect of preparation. It ensures everyone involved in the incident response process understands their specific duties and how they contribute to the overall response effort.

Let's see why the other phases wouldn't be the primary focus for reviewing roles and responsibilities:

B. Recovery: The recovery phase concentrates on restoring affected systems and data after an incident. While roles might be re-evaluated based on the incident complexity, the primary focus is on remediation efforts.

C. Lessons learned: This phase involves analyzing the incident and identifying areas for improvement in the incident response process. While roles might be reviewed as part of this analysis, it's not the main objective during the lessons learned phase.

D. Analysis: The analysis phase focuses on collecting and analyzing evidence to understand the nature and scope of the security incident. While the analyst might need to understand their own role within the analysis process, reviewing everyone's roles is a broader aspect addressed during preparation.

The preparation phase is proactive. By clearly defining roles and responsibilities beforehand, the organization can ensure a more efficient and coordinated response when a security incident occurs.

Here are some additional activities typically performed during the preparation phase:

Developing an incident response plan: This plan outlines the steps to be taken during all phases of an incident response process, including roles and responsibilities.

Conducting training: Regular training helps team members understand their roles and responsibilities, as well as the overall incident response process.

Testing the incident response plan: Testing helps identify potential gaps in the plan and ensure roles and responsibilities are well-defined and understood.

By investing time and effort into the preparation phase, including a clear definition of roles and responsibilities, organizations can significantly improve their ability to respond effectively to security incidents.

26) Out of the listed options, the most likely method for a systems administrator to implement a password policy update across all systems in an enterprise environment quickly is:

B. Pushing GPO update

Here's why GPO (Group Policy Object) updates are the best choice for this scenario:

GPO (Group Policy Objects): In a Windows domain environment, GPOs provide a centralized way to manage settings and configurations for Active Directory (AD) domain-joined computers. This includes password policies. By modifying the password policy in a GPO and applying the update, the administrator can efficiently push the new policy to all affected systems within the domain.

Let's explore why the other options wouldn't be ideal for this large-scale update:

A. Deploying PowerShell scripts: While PowerShell scripts can be used to automate tasks like password policy changes, scripting individual machines wouldn't be as efficient as leveraging GPOs for mass deployment across an enterprise environment.

C. Enabling PAP (Password Authentication Protocol): PAP is a weak authentication protocol and wouldn't be a suitable security measure for password policy updates.

D. Updating EDR profiles: Endpoint Detection and Response (EDR) software focuses on monitoring endpoints for threats. While EDR profiles might include password strength requirements, updating them wouldn't necessarily manage the group password policy across all systems.

GPOs offer a central and efficient way to enforce consistent password policies across a large number of domain-joined computers. This ensures all systems comply with the organization's security standards and reduces the risk of weak password practices.

Here are some additional benefits of using GPOs for password policy updates:

Scalability: A single GPO update can be applied to all relevant systems within the domain.

Standardization: GPOs ensure consistent password policy enforcement across all affected systems.

Centralized management: Administrators can manage password policies from a central location.

By leveraging GPOs, the systems administrator can achieve a rapid and efficient deployment of the new password policy across all enterprise systems.

27) Out of the listed options, the most secure recommendation for the security analyst to address a remote desktop service on the public network is:

B. Setting up a VPN and placing the jump server inside the firewall

Here's why a VPN and jump server implementation is the best approach:

Public network access: The remote desktop service should not be directly accessible from the public internet. Exposing a remote desktop service on the public network creates a significant security risk as it provides a direct entry point for unauthorized access attempts.

VPN and jump server: A virtual private network (VPN) creates a secure tunnel between the remote user's device and the organization's network. A jump server is a secure server within the organization's network specifically designated for accessing internal resources like remote desktops.

Here's how this approach improves security:

Reduced attack surface: The remote desktop service itself wouldn't be directly exposed to the public internet, significantly reducing the attack surface.

Controlled access: Users would need to connect to the VPN first, adding an additional layer of authentication before accessing the jump server. The jump server can then be configured to grant access only to authorized users and specific internal resources (e.g., the production network remote desktop).

Let's see why the other options wouldn't be the most secure solutions:

A. Changing the remote desktop port: While changing the port from the default (3389) might make it slightly less discoverable for attackers, it wouldn't be a foolproof security measure. Attackers can easily scan for non-standard ports as well.

C. Using a proxy for web connections: A proxy server wouldn't necessarily address the core issue of remote desktop access being available from the public internet. Malicious actors could still exploit vulnerabilities in the remote desktop service to gain access.

D. Connecting the server to the domain and increasing password length: While these practices are good security measures in general, they wouldn't address the fundamental problem of the remote desktop service being directly accessible from the public network.

By implementing a VPN and jump server architecture, the security analyst can significantly improve the security of remote desktop access and minimize the risk of unauthorized access to the production network. This approach provides a more secure and controlled access method compared to directly exposing the remote desktop service on the public internet.

28) Out of the listed options, the strategy the bank is most likely requiring vendors to implement to prevent data loss in case of a stolen laptop is:

A. Encryption at rest

Here's why encryption at rest is the best choice for this scenario:

Data loss prevention: Encryption at rest scrambles data on storage devices (like laptops) using a cryptographic key. If a laptop is stolen, the data on the device remains unreadable without the decryption key, rendering it useless to unauthorized individuals. This significantly reduces the risk of data breaches and protects sensitive information even in the event of physical device theft.

Let's explore why the other options wouldn't be as effective on their own:

B. Masking: Masking involves replacing sensitive data with fictitious characters, often used during testing or development to protect data privacy. While it might be helpful for certain purposes, it wouldn't necessarily protect data on a stolen laptop as the underlying data could potentially be recovered.

C. Data classification: Data classification involves identifying and labeling data based on its sensitivity. While this is an important security practice, it wouldn't directly prevent data loss on a stolen device.

D. Permission restrictions: Limiting access permissions to data can help prevent unauthorized access within an organization's network. However, it wouldn't necessarily protect data on a stolen laptop if the device itself isn't encrypted.

Encryption at rest provides a strong layer of protection for data stored on laptops. By scrambling the data, it ensures even if a laptop falls into the wrong hands, the information remains confidential and unusable. This is a critical security measure for organizations like banks that handle sensitive financial data and need to protect it from unauthorized access in case of device theft.

29) Out of the listed options, the scenario described most likely indicates an:

A. Insider threat

Here's why insider threat is the most fitting description:

Encrypted files: The fact that files on the database server were encrypted suggests a deliberate attempt to restrict access to the data.

Domain user access: Security logs indicating a domain user accessed the data last strengthens the case for an insider threat. Domain users are typically authorized users within an organization's network.

While other attack types are possible, they are less likely based on the given information:

B. Social engineering: Social engineering attacks typically involve tricking users into revealing credentials or granting access. While an attacker might use social engineering to gain initial access, encrypting files on a database server suggests a level of access and technical knowledge more indicative of an insider.

C. Watering-hole: Watering-hole attacks target websites frequented by a specific group of users. The focus is often on compromising user devices, not directly encrypting data on a database server.

D. Unauthorized attacker: This is a broad category, but unauthorized attackers typically wouldn't have legitimate domain user access. They would need to exploit a vulnerability or gain unauthorized access through other means before encrypting files.

Insider threats can pose a significant risk to organizations. They can leverage their authorized access and knowledge of internal systems to carry out malicious activities like data encryption or exfiltration.

Here are some additional considerations:

The specific type of insider threat could be further classified based on the attacker's motivation (e.g., disgruntled employee, financial gain).

Organizations should implement security measures to detect and mitigate insider threats, such as user activity monitoring and data loss prevention (DLP) solutions.

30) Out of the listed options, the most suitable protocol for the security analyst to enable for user authentication using smart cards is:

D. EAP-TLS (Extensible Authentication Protocol - Transport Layer Security)

Here's why EAP-TLS is the best choice for smart card authentication:

Smart card authentication: EAP-TLS is a secure authentication protocol specifically designed to work with digital certificates stored on smart cards. Smart cards provide a more secure way to store and use cryptographic keys compared to traditional passwords.

Mutual authentication: EAP-TLS supports mutual authentication, where not only the user is authenticated by the network but also the network server is authenticated by the user's smart card. This adds an extra layer of security.

Let's explore why the other options wouldn't be ideal for smart card authentication:

A. CHAP (Challenge-Handshake Authentication Protocol): CHAP is a relatively simple authentication protocol that doesn't directly support smart cards. While some variations might be used with tokens, it wouldn't be the most secure option for smart card authentication.

B. PEAP (Protected Extensible Authentication Protocol): PEAP can be used to tunnel other authentication protocols like EAP-TLS within a secure channel. However, PEAP itself doesn't directly utilize smart cards.

C. MS-CHAPv2 (Microsoft Challenge Handshake Authentication Protocol Version 2): Similar to CHAP, MS-CHAPv2 is a password-based authentication protocol that wouldn't directly leverage the security benefits of smart cards.

EAP-TLS offers a robust and secure method for user authentication using smart cards. By utilizing digital certificates stored on smart cards and supporting mutual authentication, EAP-TLS significantly enhances network access security compared to traditional password-based methods.

31) Out of the listed options, the most suitable automation technique for a system administrator to streamline account creation with accurate access and permissions is:

D. User provisioning script

Here's why user provisioning scripts are the best choice for this scenario:

User provisioning: This process automates the creation of new user accounts in various systems and applications. User provisioning scripts can be configured to set up accounts with predefined access controls and permissions based on user roles or departments. This ensures consistency and reduces the risk of manual errors that might lead to inaccurate access configurations.

Let's see why the other options wouldn't be ideal solutions for this specific task:

A. Guard rail script: Guard rail scripts are typically used

to enforce security policies or configurations across systems. While they can be helpful in ensuring certain security baselines are met during account creation, they wouldn't directly automate the provisioning process itself.

B. Ticketing workflow: Ticketing workflows can be used to manage service requests, including account creation. However, they wouldn't automate the account creation process itself. An administrator would still need to manually create the account and configure permissions after a ticket is approved.

C. Escalation script: Escalation scripts are designed to automatically escalate incidents or issues that meet certain criteria. They wouldn't directly address the task of automating user account creation with accurate permissions.

User provisioning scripts offer several advantages for streamlining account creation:

Efficiency: They automate repetitive tasks, saving administrators time and effort.

Consistency: They ensure new accounts are created with the same permissions every time, reducing the risk of human error.

Security: They can be configured to enforce security best practices, such as requiring strong passwords or limiting access based on the principle of least privilege.

By implementing user provisioning scripts, the system administrator can address the management team's concerns about inconsistent access control for new accounts. User provisioning automates the creation process and ensures new accounts have the appropriate permissions based on predefined rules, improving efficiency and security.

32) Out of the listed options, the one used to measure the

vulnerability criticality in a quantitative manner is:

B. CVSS (Common Vulnerability Scoring System)

Here's why CVSS is the best choice:

CVSS (Common Vulnerability Scoring System): This system assigns a score (ranging from 0.0 to 10.0) to a vulnerability based on several factors including exploitability, potential impact, and scope. The higher the CVSS score, the more critical the vulnerability is considered. This provides a standardized way to assess vulnerability severity and prioritize remediation efforts.

Let's explore why the other options aren't used for quantitative vulnerability measurement:

A. CVE (Common Vulnerabilities and Exposures): CVE is a database that assigns a unique identifier to each known vulnerability. While CVE entries may include severity ratings, they are not quantitative and can be subjective. CVSS builds upon CVE by providing a more objective scoring system.

C. CIA (Confidentiality, Integrity, Availability): CIA triad is a security model that represents the core security objectives of protecting information confidentiality, integrity, and availability. CVSS takes these objectives into account when scoring vulnerabilities, but it's not the CIA model itself that provides the quantitative measurement.

D. CERT (Coordination Center for Emergency Response Teams): CERT is an organization that coordinates vulnerability information sharing and response efforts. While CERT may publish vulnerability information that includes severity ratings, CVSS is the specific scoring system used for quantitative measurement.

33) Out of the listed options, the scenario described most likely indicates an:

D. Insider threat

Here's why insider threat is the most fitting description:

Remote access after-hours: The user logged in outside of typical work hours, suggesting potential attempts to avoid detection.

Transferring data: The user transferred a significant amount of data to a personal device, which could be exfiltrating sensitive information.

While other possibilities exist, they are less likely based on the given details:

A. Penetration testing: Penetration testing is usually authorized and conducted during agreed-upon times. It wouldn't typically involve transferring data to personal devices.

B. Phishing campaign: Phishing campaigns target user credentials, not direct data exfiltration by authorized users with remote access.

C. External audit: External audits are typically conducted with the organization's knowledge and wouldn't involve unauthorized data transfers.

Insider threats pose a significant risk because they have authorized access to systems and data. Their knowledge of internal controls can make their activities more difficult to detect.

Here are some additional considerations:

The administrator should investigate the user's activity further to determine the exact nature of the data transfer and potential consequences.

Organizations should implement measures to detect and mitigate insider threats, such as user activity monitoring and data loss prevention (DLP) solutions.

34) Out of the listed options, the most suitable choice for dynamic environments with frequent changes is:

B. Containers

Here's why containers are the best fit for dynamic environments:

Dynamic environments: Containers are lightweight and portable, making them ideal for dynamic environments where applications and configurations need to be deployed and scaled quickly. They can be easily spun up or down based on changing requirements.

Frequent changes: Containers allow for isolation and versioning of application dependencies. This enables developers to make frequent changes to applications without affecting other applications or the underlying system.

Let's see why the other options wouldn't be the most suitable for this scenario:

A. RTOS (Real-Time Operating System): RTOSes are lightweight operating systems designed for deterministic performance, which is crucial for real-time applications. While they can be efficient, they typically don't offer the same level of flexibility and isolation as containers when it comes to frequent changes in dynamic environments.

C. Embedded systems: Embedded systems are computer systems designed for specific purposes within a larger device. While containers can be used within embedded systems, "embedded systems" itself isn't a technology for managing frequent changes in dynamic environments.

D. SCADA (Supervisory Control and Data Acquisition): SCADA systems are used for industrial process control. While SCADA systems might leverage containers in some cases, they are domain-specific systems and not generally the primary technology for managing frequent changes in dynamic environments.

Containers provide several advantages for dynamic environments:

Isolation: Applications running in containers are isolated from each other and the underlying system. This reduces the risk of conflicts and simplifies troubleshooting.

Portability: Containers can be easily moved between different environments (development, testing, production) without modification.

Scalability: Containers can be quickly scaled up or down to meet changing resource demands.

By utilizing containers, organizations can achieve greater agility and flexibility in managing applications and configurations within dynamic environments with frequent changes.

35) Out of the listed options, the strategy a company procuring cyber insurance to mitigate risks identified in the risk register represents is:

C. Transfer

Here's why transferring risk is the most relevant choice:

Cyber insurance: When a company purchases cyber insurance, they are essentially transferring the financial risk associated with cyberattacks to the insurance provider. In exchange for a premium, the insurance company agrees to cover certain costs incurred in the event of a cyberattack, such as data breach remediation or legal fees.

Let's explore why the other options wouldn't be the perfect fit in this scenario:

A. Avoid: Avoiding cyber risk altogether might not be practical in today's digital world. Most businesses rely on technology and face some level of cyber risk.

B. Mitigate: While cyber insurance can be a part of a risk mitigation strategy, it doesn't eliminate the risk entirely. Organizations should still implement security controls and other measures to reduce the likelihood and impact of cyberattacks.

D. Accept: Accepting cyber risk without any mitigation or transfer strategies would leave the company fully exposed to the financial consequences of a cyberattack.

Cyber insurance acts as a risk transfer mechanism. By paying premiums, the company transfers some of the financial burden associated with cyberattacks to the insurance provider. However, it's important to note that cyber insurance policies typically have limitations and exclusions, and companies should still implement appropriate security measures to minimize their cyber risk.

36) Out of the listed options, the most cost-effective, cloud-based application hosting solution for a systems administrator is:

C. Serverless framework

Here's why serverless frameworks are the best fit for this scenario:

Cost-effective: Serverless frameworks eliminate the need for server provisioning and maintenance. You only pay for the resources your application uses when it's executing code. This can be significantly more cost-effective compared to traditional hosting options where you pay for a fixed amount of server resources regardless of usage.

Cloud-based: Serverless frameworks operate within the cloud infrastructure of providers like AWS Lambda, Azure Functions, or Google Cloud Functions.

Let's see why the other options wouldn't be ideal solutions for cost-effective application hosting:

A. SDN (Software-Defined Networking): SDN is a technology for managing and controlling network traffic. While it can be used in cloud environments, it's not directly related to application hosting.

B. Type 1 hypervisor: A type 1 hypervisor allows virtualization of multiple operating systems on a single physical server. This can be a cost-effective way to host multiple applications, but it still requires managing the underlying server infrastructure.

D. SD-WAN (Software-Defined Wide Area Network): SD-WAN optimizes internet connectivity across geographically distributed locations. While it can be beneficial for cloud deployments, it's not directly related to application hosting itself.

Serverless frameworks offer several advantages for cost-effective application hosting:

Scalability: Serverless applications can automatically scale based on demand, eliminating the need to manually provision resources.

Reduced complexity: Serverless frameworks handle server management tasks, allowing developers to focus on application logic.

By leveraging a serverless framework, the systems administrator can achieve a cost-effective and scalable solution for cloud-based application hosting. They won't need to worry about server infrastructure management and can benefit from automatic scaling based on application usage.

37) Out of the listed options, the access control most likely inhibiting the user's ability to transfer the patch is:

D. Least privilege

Here's why least privilege is the best fit:

Least privilege principle: This principle dictates that users should be granted only the minimum permissions necessary to perform their jobs. In this scenario, the user attempting to transfer the patch might not have the necessary "write" permissions to modify the critical system.

Let's explore why the other options are less likely to be the culprit:

A. Attribute-based access control (ABAC): While ABAC can restrict access based on various attributes, it's not typically used to control file transfer operations in this context.

B. Time of day access control: This type of access control restricts access based on the time of day. It wouldn't necessarily prevent the user from transferring the patch altogether, only during specific time windows.

C. Role-based access control (RBAC): RBAC assigns permissions based on user roles. If the user's role doesn't include patching duties, RBAC could restrict their ability to transfer the patch. However, least privilege is a more fundamental principle that applies across various access control models, including RBAC.

The principle of least privilege ensures that users have only the access they need to perform their tasks. This reduces the risk of unauthorized modifications or accidental damage to critical systems. In this scenario, the user likely lacks the necessary write permissions to transfer the patch file, which could be due to least privilege being enforced.

38) Out of the listed options, the most likely type of infection present on the systems based on the .ryk extension is:

D. Ransomware

Here's why ransomware is the best fit:

.ryk file extension: Ransomware is a type of malware that encrypts a victim's files and demands a ransom payment for decryption. The .ryk extension is a common extension used by some ransomware variants, including the Ryuk strain. When ransomware encrypts files, it often appends a specific extension to the filename to indicate the encryption and potentially identify the ransomware variant.

Let's explore why the other options are less likely:

A. Virus: While viruses can replicate and spread, they typically don't encrypt files and demand ransom payments.

B. Trojan: Trojans are malicious programs that disguise themselves as legitimate software. Their primary function can vary, but encrypting files and demanding ransom isn't a common characteristic of Trojans.

C. Spyware: Spyware is designed to steal sensitive information from a victim's device. While it might interact with files, it wouldn't typically encrypt them and display messages related to a specific file extension.

The presence of a common ransomware extension (like .ryk) across user workstations and servers suggests a widespread encryption event, which is a hallmark of ransomware attacks.

Here are some additional considerations:

The administrator should immediately isolate infected systems to prevent further spread of the ransomware.

They should investigate the specific ransomware variant and determine if decryption tools are available.

Organizations should have backups in place to restore encrypted files in case decryption isn't possible.

39) Correct answer: C. Least privilege.

This principle ensures that employees have only the minimum level of access necessary to perform their job functions, reducing the risk of inadvertently installing malware due to excessive permissions.

40) Out of the listed options, the technology that can be used to detect potential attacker actions without impacting production servers is:

A. Honeypot

Here's why a honeypot is the best choice for this scenario:

Honeypot: A honeypot is a decoy system designed to mimic a real production server. It's deployed in a separate environment and attracts attackers. Since it's isolated from production systems, security teams can monitor attacker activities within the honeypot environment without affecting real servers. By analyzing these activities, they can gain insights into attacker techniques and tactics, allowing them to improve overall security posture.

Let's explore why the other options wouldn't be ideal for detecting attacker actions without impacting production servers:

B. Video surveillance: While video surveillance can be used for security purposes, it wouldn't directly detect attacker actions on servers. It might be helpful in identifying physical security breaches, but it wouldn't provide insights into network traffic or attacker behavior.

C. Zero Trust: Zero Trust is a security model that emphasizes continuous verification before granting access. While it's a valuable security principle, it wouldn't be a specific technology used for detection purposes in this context.

D. Geofencing: Geofencing defines virtual geographic boundaries. While it can be used for location-based security measures, it wouldn't directly detect attacker actions on servers.

Honeypots offer a safe and controlled environment to observe attacker behavior. By mimicking production systems, they lure attackers away from real servers and provide valuable insights into potential threats without disrupting critical operations.

Here are some additional benefits of honeypots:

Early threat detection: Honeypots can help identify new attack techniques before they impact production systems.

Improved security awareness: Analyzing honeypot data can help security teams understand attacker motivations and improve overall security strategies.

By deploying honeypots, organizations can proactively detect potential threats and enhance their cybersecurity posture.

41) Out of the listed options, following a legal hold request due to a security breach lawsuit, the security team will most likely be required to:

B. Retain any communications related to the security breach until further notice.

Here's why option B is the most fitting response to a legal hold:

Legal hold: When a lawsuit is filed, a legal hold can be issued to preserve any relevant evidence. This typically includes all communications related to the security breach, such as emails, logs, reports, and investigative findings.

Let's see why the other options wouldn't be the most likely actions:

A. Retain emails between security and affected customers for 30 days: The legal hold would likely encompass all relevant communications, not just a specific timeframe or recipient group. 30 days might be too short depending on the lawsuit and legal proceedings.

C. Retain communications between security members: While internal security team communication might be relevant, the legal hold would likely cover a broader range of communications related to the breach, including those with external parties.

D. Retain all emails from the company to affected customers for an indefinite period: The legal hold would focus on relevant communications related to the breach, not necessarily all communication with affected customers. Additionally, an indefinite hold might not be practical or legal depending on data retention policies.

The primary purpose of a legal hold in this scenario is to ensure all potentially relevant evidence related to the security breach is preserved for the lawsuit. This may include communication with various parties, logs, and investigative data. The security team should work closely with the company's legal team to understand the specific requirements of the legal hold and ensure they are met.

42) Out of the listed options, the most suitable solution for the administrator to restrict access to confidential data quickly following an audit finding is:

D. Access control lists (ACLs)

Here's why ACLs are the best choice in this scenario:

Access control lists (ACLs): ACLs are a mechanism for controlling access to resources like files and folders. They specify which users or groups have permission to read, write, modify, or delete the data. By modifying the ACLs on the confidential data folder, the administrator can quickly restrict access to authorized users only.

Let's explore why the other options wouldn't be the most effective for this specific task:

A. Group Policy (GPO): While Group Policy can be used to manage user permissions, it might not be the quickest solution for this scenario. Implementing and enforcing GPOs can take time, depending on the complexity of the environment.

B. Content filtering: Content filtering typically focuses on network traffic and wouldn't directly control access to data stored on a file server.

C. Data loss prevention (DLP): DLP solutions are valuable for preventing unauthorized data exfiltration, but they might not be the most suitable option for quickly restricting access to existing data on a server. Implementing and configuring DLP solutions can also involve some lead time.

ACLs offer a granular and efficient way to control access to files and folders. By modifying the ACLs on the confidential data folder, the administrator can immediately restrict access to authorized users only, addressing the audit finding promptly.

Here are some additional considerations:

The administrator should review the ACLs for other sensitive data on the server to ensure appropriate access controls are in place.

They should determine the root cause of why all users had access to confidential data and implement measures to prevent similar issues in the future. This might involve implementing user roles and least privilege principles for access control.

43) The common VoIP-associated vulnerabilities are:

A. SPIM (Spam over Internet Messaging): SPIM is a type of spam targeting users of instant messaging (IM) services, including VoIP systems. It can be used to send unsolicited messages, advertisements, or malicious links to users.

B. Vishing (Voice Phishing): Vishing is a form of phishing that uses voice communication to deceive individuals into divulging sensitive information, such as financial details or personal data, by pretending to be a legitimate entity.

Explanation:

SPIM can exploit VoIP systems by sending unsolicited messages that may include malicious content or links, potentially leading to security breaches.

Vishing specifically targets users of VoIP services by using voice calls to trick individuals into providing confidential information, making it a direct threat to VoIP security.

Other options such as VLAN hopping, phishing, DHCP snooping, and tailgating are not specific to VoIP vulnerabilities:

C. VLAN hopping: This is a network attack that allows an attacker to gain access to traffic on other VLANs.

D. Phishing: This is a general term for fraudulent attempts to obtain sensitive information via email, not specific to VoIP.

E. DHCP snooping: This is a network security feature that monitors DHCP traffic, not directly related to VoIP.

F. Tailgating: This refers to unauthorized physical access to a secure area by following an authorized person, unrelated to VoIP systems.

44) Out of the listed options, the most effective practice to prevent insider-introduced malicious code is:

D. Peer review and approval

Here's why peer review is most effective:

Human Analysis: Peer review involves other developers examining the code. This allows for a fresh perspective to identify suspicious code sections or functionalities that might be intentionally malicious.

Intentional Code Detection: Automated code scanning (option A) might miss cleverly hidden malicious code, while peer review can raise red flags about unusual functionalities or code that deviates from coding standards.

Discourages Malicious Intent: Knowing their code will be scrutinized by peers can deter developers from intentionally introducing malicious code.

While the other options offer some security benefits:

Code scanning for vulnerabilities (A): This is a good practice to identify general vulnerabilities, but it might not catch well-disguised malicious code.

Open-source component usage (B): Open-source components can introduce vulnerabilities, but it's not a direct prevention method against insider threats.

Quality assurance testing (C): QA testing focuses on functionality, not necessarily malicious code.

Therefore, for insider threat prevention, peer review with its human analysis and potential deterrence effect is the most effective approach.

45) Out of the listed options, the vulnerability most specific to hardware is:

A. Firmware version

Here's why firmware version can be a hardware vulnerability:

Hardware Integration: Firmware is low-level software that directly interacts with hardware components. Vulnerabilities in specific firmware versions can expose security holes in the hardware itself. This can be due to programming flaws or design weaknesses in the hardware that the firmware interacts with.

For the other options:

Buffer overflow (B), SQL injection (C), Cross-site scripting (D): These are software vulnerabilities that can be exploited in various software programs, not specific to hardware. They can be present in operating systems, web applications, or other software.

46) The best approach to managing a critical business application on a legacy server depends on your long-term goals and resources. Here's a breakdown of the options to help you decide:

C. Hardening: This is a strong initial step. Hardening involves securing the server by:

Minimizing unnecessary software and services running.

Applying the latest security patches to the operating system and applications.

Configuring strong passwords and access controls.

Implementing firewalls and intrusion detection systems.

Hardening is essential to mitigate vulnerabilities on the legacy server, but it might not be the long-term solution.

A. Segmentation: This involves isolating the server on a separate network segment with restricted access. It helps prevent attacks spreading to other systems but doesn't address potential vulnerabilities within the legacy application itself.

B. Isolation: Similar to segmentation, isolation focuses on physically separating the server from the main network. This can be an extra layer of security, but it doesn't address the inherent limitations of outdated hardware or software.

D. Decommissioning: This is the most future-proof option, but requires careful planning. It involves migrating the application to a more modern platform, such as a cloud environment or a newer server with better security features. Decommissioning offers long-term benefits like improved performance, scalability, and reduced maintenance costs, but requires upfront investment and potential downtime during migration.

Here's how to choose the best approach:

Evaluate the application's criticality: How crucial is this application to your business operations?

Assess your budget and resources: Can you invest in modernization (decommissioning) or are you looking for a more immediate solution (hardening)?

Consider the future: Do you plan to continue using this application long-term?

In many cases, hardening the server is a good first step, but decommissioning to a modern platform is the most sustainable approach for critical business applications in the long run.

47) The document that includes information on uptime guarantees for a service provider's hosted security services is:

D. SLA

Here's why an SLA is the most relevant document:

Service Level Agreement (SLA): An SLA is a formal agreement between a service provider and a client that outlines the expected service levels, including uptime guarantees, performance metrics, and service credits for downtime exceeding agreed-upon thresholds.

While the other documents might be relevant during the contracting process, they don't specifically address service level guarantees:

Memorandum of Agreement (MOA): An MOA is a high-level agreement outlining the intent to collaborate but doesn't typically specify technical details like uptime.

Statement of Work (SOW): An SOW details the specific tasks or services to be delivered but might not explicitly mention uptime guarantees unless it's a critical aspect of the service.

Memorandum of Understanding (MOU): An MOU is similar to an MOA and focuses on general cooperation, not technical service level specifics.

Therefore, the SLA is the binding document that would specify the minimum uptime of 99.99% for the hosted security services.

48) Out of the listed options, the most suitable logs for the analyst to investigate the executable are:

A. Endpoint logs

Here's why endpoint logs are the best choice:

Endpoint logs: These logs capture detailed information about activities on a specific device, including the execution of programs and processes. They would likely contain details about the specific executable running on the employee's laptop, such as the filename, path, timestamps, and potentially even command-line arguments used when the program was executed.

The other options might provide some information but

wouldn't be as comprehensive:

Network logs (C): Network logs show network traffic details like source and destination IP addresses, ports used, and potentially some application data. While they might indicate suspicious network activity related to the executable, they wouldn't reveal details about the executable itself.

Application logs (B): Application logs are specific to individual applications and might provide some details if the suspicious executable is a known application. However, for a potentially malicious executable, application logs might be limited or non-existent.

IPS/IDS logs (D): Intrusion Prevention/Detection System logs provide information about security events detected by the system. These logs might indicate that the network traffic triggered an IPS/IDS rule, but wouldn't necessarily provide details about the specific executable running on the endpoint.

Therefore, endpoint logs offer the most granular details about the executable in question, allowing the security analyst to effectively investigate its legitimacy.

49) Out of the listed options, the most crucial first step for the security administrator implementing a DLP solution is:

C. Apply classifications to the data

Here's why data classification is essential:

Understanding What to Protect: Classifying data helps identify what information is considered sensitive and needs DLP protection. This includes customer data, financial information, intellectual property, etc. Without classification, the DLP solution wouldn't know what data to monitor and protect.

While the other options might be part of a DLP strategy, they should come after data classification:

Blocking cloud storage websites (A): This could be a potential action based on DLP rules, but it's a blunt approach that might hinder legitimate cloud storage usage. Classifying data allows for more targeted rules that focus on the data itself, not just the destination.

Blocking outgoing email attachments (B): Similar to blocking websites, this is an action based on DLP rules. Data classification helps define which attachments containing sensitive data should be blocked.

Removing all user permissions (D): This is an overly restrictive approach. DLP allows for granular control. Data classification helps identify which users or groups need restricted access to sensitive data.

Therefore, classifying data provides the foundation for configuring effective DLP rules to prevent customer data exfiltration.

50) The attacker is using the technique of D. Whaling.

Here's why whaling is the most fitting option:

Whaling: This is a type of social engineering attack that specifically targets high-level executives like CEOs. Attackers impersonate them to manipulate employees into taking actions that benefit the attacker, such as transferring funds or revealing sensitive information.

The scenario describes an attacker impersonating a CEO (high-level executive) to trick an employee (target) into purchasing gift cards (action benefiting the attacker).

Here's why the other options are not as applicable:

Smishing (A): This involves phishing attempts via SMS text messages. While social engineering, it doesn't necessarily target high-level executives.

Disinformation (B): Disinformation refers to spreading false or misleading information, which isn't the attacker's primary goal here.

Impersonating (C): Impersonation is a broad term, but whaling is a specific type of impersonation attack targeting high-profile individuals.

51) The most appropriate next step after a vulnerability assessment and remediation is to:

D. Rescan the network.

Here's why rescanning the network is crucial:

Validation of Remediation: Rescanning allows you to verify if the vulnerabilities identified earlier have been effectively addressed by the operations team. It helps confirm that the remediation efforts were successful and the vulnerabilities are no longer present.

While the other options might be part of a security process, they don't directly follow a vulnerability assessment and remediation cycle:

A. Initiate a penetration test: Penetration testing is a simulated attack to exploit vulnerabilities and assess the effectiveness of security controls. It can be a valuable next step, but it's ideal to perform it after confirming the remediation through a rescan.

B. Submit a report: A report summarizing the findings of the vulnerability assessment is important, but it's typically done after the remediation and rescanning process.

C. Conduct an audit: A security audit is a broader examination of an organization's security posture, including policies, procedures, and technical controls. It might be conducted periodically, but a vulnerability assessment focuses on specific technical vulnerabilities.

Therefore, rescanning the network after remediation is the essential step to ensure the vulnerabilities have been addressed and the network security posture is improved.

52) The security technique described in the policy is A. Input validation.

Here's why input validation is the best explanation:

Sanitizing User Input: The policy describes using regular expressions to remove special characters from user input in forms. This is a common technique in input validation to prevent malicious code injection or manipulation of data submitted through forms. By removing these special characters, the organization aims to prevent attackers from exploiting vulnerabilities in the web application.

Regular expressions are a tool used to define patterns for searching and manipulating text, making them suitable for validating user input.

Let's analyze why the other options are not as relevant:

B. Static code analysis: Static code analysis involves examining code without running it. While it can identify potential vulnerabilities, it wouldn't typically focus on removing specific characters from user input during runtime, as described in the policy.

C. Code debugging: Code debugging is the process of identifying and fixing errors in code. The policy doesn't mention fixing errors, but rather preventing them through input validation.

D. Identify embedded keys: Embedded keys are typically used for encryption or licensing purposes. The policy describes removing characters from user input, not searching for specific embedded keys.

Therefore, based on the focus on sanitizing user input with regular expressions, input validation (A) is the most fitting explanation for the security technique adopted by the organization.

53) Out of the listed options, three choices are suitable for describing technical security controls:

B. Sometimes called logical security controls: This accurately reflects an alternative term for technical security controls. Logical controls refer to the policies and procedures implemented through technology, as opposed to physical security controls that protect physical assets.

C. Executed by computer systems (instead of people): Technical controls are automated and rely on computer systems to function. Firewalls, intrusion detection systems, and encryption are examples that operate without human intervention.

E. Implemented with technology: This is a core aspect of technical controls. They leverage technology like software, hardware, or firmware to safeguard systems and data.

Let's break down why the other options are not suitable for

technical security controls:

A. Focused on protecting material assets: While security is comprehensive, technical controls often focus on protecting digital assets and information systems, not necessarily physical materials. Physical security controls address that area.

D. Also known as administrative controls: Administrative controls are policies, procedures, and guidelines established by management to define security practices. These are enforced through technical controls or human actions.

F. Primarily implemented and executed by people (as opposed to computer systems): This describes administrative controls, where people play a primary role. Technical controls are automated and function independently.

54) Out of the listed options, three choices are examples of technical security controls:

B. Encryption: Encryption scrambles data using algorithms and keys, making it unreadable to unauthorized users. This protects sensitive information at rest (stored on devices) and in transit (transferred over networks).

D. IDSs (Intrusion Detection Systems): These are software applications that monitor network traffic and system activity for suspicious behavior that might indicate an attack. They can trigger alerts or take automated actions to stop intrusions.

F. Firewalls: Firewalls act as barriers between trusted and untrusted networks, controlling incoming and outgoing traffic based on predefined security rules. They can help prevent unauthorized access to internal systems.

Let's look at why the other options are not technical security controls:

A. Security audits: Security audits are methodical reviews of an organization's security posture. While they identify areas for improvement in technical controls, they are not technical controls themselves.

C. Organizational security policy: This is an administrative control that defines security best practices and user behavior. It outlines how technical controls should be used.

E. Configuration management: This is a process of maintaining consistent configurations for IT systems and devices. While it can support technical security controls, it's not directly a security control itself.

55) Out of the listed options, three choices describe the characteristic features of managerial security controls:

A. Also known as administrative controls: Managerial security controls are synonymous with administrative controls. They establish guidelines, procedures, and policies to guide security practices within an organization.

C. Focused on reducing the risk of security incidents: A core objective of managerial security controls is to mitigate security risks. These controls define best practices, user behavior expectations, and incident response procedures, all aimed at minimizing the likelihood and impact of security incidents.

E. Documented in written policies: Managerial security controls are typically documented in written policies, access control lists, and security awareness training materials. These documents communicate expectations and guide user behavior to uphold security standards.

Let's explore why the other options are not characteristic features of managerial security controls:

B. Sometimes referred to as logical security controls: Logical security controls are implemented through technology, while managerial controls focus on policies and procedures. However, managerial controls can define how logical security controls are used.

D. Executed by computer systems (instead of people): Managerial security controls rely on people to implement and enforce them. They provide the framework for user behavior and security practices.

F. Focused on protecting material assets: While security is comprehensive, managerial controls often emphasize protecting information systems and data, although they can encompass physical security policies as well.

56) Out of the listed options, three choices are examples of managerial security controls:

C. Organizational security policy: This is a formal document outlining the security rules, procedures, and expectations for users within an organization. It defines acceptable use of resources, password policies, data handling practices, and reporting procedures for security incidents.

D. Risk assessments: Managerial security controls involve identifying and mitigating security risks. Risk assessments are a systematic process of evaluating vulnerabilities, potential threats, and the impact of security incidents. This helps prioritize security measures and allocate resources effectively.

E. Security awareness training: Educating users about security best practices and potential threats is crucial. Security awareness training programs equip users with the knowledge and skills to identify suspicious activity, avoid security pitfalls, and report incidents appropriately.

Let's look at why the other options are not managerial security controls:

A. Configuration management: While configuration management can support security by ensuring consistent system configurations, it's a technical process, not a policy or procedure.

B. Data backups: Data backups are a technical security measure that ensures data recovery in case of incidents. It's not a policy or user behavior guideline.

57) Out of the listed options, three choices are suitable for describing operational security controls (OPSEC):

B. Focused on the day-to-day procedures of an organization: OPSEC emphasizes the ongoing practices and behaviors that influence the security posture. This includes procedures for handling classified information, access controls, physical security measures, and user activity monitoring.

E. Focused on managing risk: A core principle of OPSEC is to identify, analyze, and mitigate risks to information security. Operational procedures are established to minimize the potential for unauthorized disclosure, modification, or disruption of critical information.

F. Primarily implemented and executed by people (as opposed to computer systems): Unlike technical controls that are automated, OPSEC controls rely on people to follow established procedures, maintain situational awareness, and report suspicious activity.

Let's break down why the other options are not suitable for describing operational security controls:

A. Also known as administrative controls: Administrative controls define security policies and procedures, but OPSEC focuses on the implementation and execution of those controls through day-to-day activities.

C. Executed by computer systems (instead of people): OPSEC controls are primarily human-driven, while technical controls leverage computer systems for automated enforcement.

D. Used to ensure that the equipment continues to work as specified: While equipment functionality is important, OPSEC is more focused on information security and mitigating risks to data confidentiality, integrity, and availability.

58) The operational security controls from the given list are:

B. Configuration management: This involves managing the configurations of systems and devices to ensure they are set up securely and in accordance with organizational policies.

C. System backups: Regular backups of systems and data are part of operational controls to ensure data can be recovered in case of a security incident or system failure.

E. Patch management: This involves managing the process of applying patches and updates to systems and software to address vulnerabilities and ensure they are up-to-date with security fixes.

A, D. Risk assessments and authentication protocols are more closely associated with administrative or technical security controls rather than operational controls.

59) The option that describes security controls aimed at physical asset protection is:

B. Physical security controls

Here's why physical security controls are the most fitting choice:

Physical Asset Protection: These controls focus on safeguarding tangible assets like buildings, equipment, data centers, and other physical resources from unauthorized access, theft, damage, or destruction. They involve a combination of physical barriers, access control systems, security personnel, and environmental controls.

Let's analyze why the other options are not as relevant:

A. Managerial security controls: These controls focus on policies and procedures, not physical barriers or access control systems.

C. Technical security controls: While some technical controls can support physical security (e.g., security cameras), technical controls are broader and encompass data security measures as well.

D. Operational security controls: These controls focus on day-to-day procedures and user behavior, not physical security measures like fences or security guards.

60) Out of the listed options, three choices are not considered physical security controls:

C. Data backups: Data backups are a technical security measure that ensures data recovery in case of incidents. They are not physical barriers or access control methods.

E. Firewalls: Firewalls are a technical security control that filters network traffic based on security rules. They don't provide physical protection for assets.

G. Asset management: Asset management is an administrative process that tracks and manages IT assets. While it can be important for security, it's not a physical security control.

Let's look why the other options are physical security controls:

A. Lighting: Proper lighting can deter intruders and improve visibility for security cameras.

B. Access control vestibules: These are secured entryways that require separate authorization to enter after passing through the initial entry point. They are a physical access control measure.

D. Fencing/Bollards/Barricades: These physical barriers create a perimeter to restrict access to specific areas.

F. Security guards: Security guards provide physical presence to deter crime, monitor activity, and enforce security policies.

61) The examples of preventive security controls are:

A. Encryption: Prevents unauthorized access to data by encrypting it, ensuring that only authorized parties can decrypt and access it.

D. Firewalls: Act as a barrier between a trusted internal network and untrusted external networks, blocking unauthorized access while permitting legitimate communication.

F. AV software: Antivirus software helps prevent malware infections by detecting and removing malicious software from systems.

B, C, E. IDS (Intrusion Detection System), sensors, and warning signs are not typically considered preventive controls. IDS detects and responds to potential security threats, sensors can be part of a monitoring or detection system, and warning signs provide awareness but do not actively prevent unauthorized access or attacks.

62) The examples of deterrent security controls are:

A. Warning signs: These indicate the presence of security measures and warn potential intruders of the consequences of unauthorized access.

C. Lighting: Proper lighting can deter intruders by increasing the perceived risk of being detected.

F. Fencing/Bollards: Physical barriers such as fencing and bollards can deter unauthorized access by making it more difficult for intruders to breach the perimeter.

B, D, E. Sensors, video surveillance, and security audits are not typically considered deterrent controls. Sensors and video surveillance are more related to detection and monitoring, while security audits are part of a broader security management process.

63) The following options describe detective security controls:

B. Log monitoring: Monitoring system logs for suspicious activity to detect potential security incidents.

D. Security audits: Assessing security measures and controls to identify weaknesses or vulnerabilities.

E. CCTV (Closed-Circuit Television): Using video surveillance to monitor and record activities for security purposes.

F. IDS (Intrusion Detection System): Monitoring network or system activities for signs of malicious activities or policy violations.

G. Vulnerability scanning: Scanning systems or networks to identify and assess potential vulnerabilities that could be exploited by attackers.

64) Out of the listed options, three describe corrective security controls:

A. IRPs (Incident Response Plans): These plans outline the procedures for responding to security incidents. They define roles, responsibilities, communication protocols, and actions to be taken when a security incident is detected. IRPs are crucial for corrective actions to contain an ongoing incident, minimize damage, and restore systems.

C. Backups and system recovery: In the aftermath of a security incident, backups allow for restoring affected systems and data to a known good state. Recovery procedures are essential for corrective actions to bring operations back online and minimize downtime.

E. Forensic analysis: After a security incident, forensic analysis involves collecting and examining digital evidence to determine the root cause of the incident, identify the attacker's methods, and gather evidence for potential legal action. Forensic analysis findings inform corrective actions to improve security posture and prevent similar incidents in the future.

Let's explore why the other options are not corrective security controls:

B. Log monitoring: While log monitoring is a detective control used to identify potential incidents, it's not a corrective action itself.

D. DRPs (Disaster Recovery Plans): DRPs are broader plans that encompass various disruptive events, not just security incidents. While they might overlap with incident response in some scenarios, DRPs focus on overall business continuity and recovery, not specifically on security breaches.

65) The options (A, C, D, E, and F) all accurately describe compensating security controls.

Here's a summary of why these options are considered compensating security controls:

A. Temporary service disablement: This mitigates risk by removing a vulnerable service while a permanent fix is developed.

C. MFA (Multi-Factor Authentication): While generally a strong control, it can be compensating if used to address a specific weakness in password complexity.

D. Backup power systems: In this context, it compensates for the potential security risk caused by a power outage.

E. Sandboxing: When used to analyze suspicious code that might exploit an unpatched vulnerability, it becomes a compensating control.

F. Temporary port blocking: This mitigates the risk of exploiting a vulnerability on a specific port while a permanent solution is implemented.

Compensating security controls are important because they provide a temporary solution to mitigate risks while a more permanent security fix is being developed or implemented. They acknowledge that a vulnerability exists and take steps to reduce the likelihood of it being exploited.

66) The statement is: "Directive security controls" is a term used to describe security controls that are implemented through policies and procedures.

A. True

This statement is accurate. Directive security controls are indeed implemented through policies and procedures.

Here's why:

Directive Controls Focus on Guidance: They provide instructions and mandates for security practices within an organization. These instructions are typically documented in policies, standards, and procedures.

Examples: Policies outlining acceptable use of resources, password complexity requirements, data handling procedures, and incident response protocols are all examples of directive security controls.

By establishing clear expectations and guidelines, directive security controls play a crucial role in shaping an organization's overall security posture.

67) The terms that are examples of directive security controls are:

A. IRP (Incident Response Plan): A plan outlining the steps to be taken in response to a security incident.

B. AUP (Acceptable Use Policy): A policy that defines acceptable use of company resources, including computers and networks, by employees.

C, D, E. IDS (Intrusion Detection System), MFA (Multi-Factor Authentication), and IPS (Intrusion Prevention System) are not examples of directive controls. IDS and IPS are technical controls, while MFA is an authentication control.

68) Out of the listed options, the term that describes the fundamental principles of information security is:

D. CIA

Here's why CIA stands out as a foundational concept:

CIA Triad: CIA stands for Confidentiality, Integrity, and Availability. This triad represents the core objectives of information security:

Confidentiality: Ensuring information is accessible only to authorized users.

Integrity: Maintaining the accuracy and completeness of data and systems.

Availability: Guaranteeing authorized users have timely access to information and systems.

These principles form the basis for developing and implementing various security controls to protect information assets.

Let's break down why the other options are not fundamental principles of information security:

A. PKI (Public Key Infrastructure): PKI is a technical framework for secure electronic communication using encryption and digital signatures. It's a tool used to achieve information security but not a core principle itself.

B. AAA (Authentication, Authorization, and Accounting): AAA is a security framework that defines how users are verified (authentication), granted access (authorization), and their activities are tracked (accounting). It's a control mechanism but not a fundamental principle.

C. GDPR (General Data Protection Regulation): GDPR is a European Union regulation that governs data privacy and protection for individuals within the EU. While data protection is a crucial aspect of information security, GDPR is a specific regulation rather than a universal principle.

69) The statement is: "Non-repudiation refers to the inability to deny responsibility for an action. In data security, it's ensures confidentiality, integrity, and origin of data."

B. False

While non-repudiation is important in data security, it's not directly related to confidentiality, integrity, and origin of data on its own.

Here's why:

Non-repudiation Focuses on Accountability: It ensures that someone cannot deny performing a particular action. This is crucial in scenarios like digital signatures or financial transactions, where it's important to prove who initiated the action.

Let's break down the CIA triad mentioned previously:

Confidentiality: Ensures information is accessible only to authorized users.

Integrity: Maintains the accuracy and completeness of data and systems.

Availability: Guarantees authorized users have timely access to information and systems.

Non-repudiation doesn't directly address these aspects. However, it can be complementary to them:

Non-repudiation and Integrity: In some cases, non-repudiation can support data integrity. For example, a digital signature with non-repudiation capabilities can help prove that data wasn't tampered with after it was signed.

Here's a corrected statement:

Non-repudiation, along with other security controls, can help ensure the confidentiality, integrity, and accountability of data.

70) The concept of non-repudiation is most accurately described by:

A. Digital certificate: A digital certificate is a secure electronic document that verifies the identity of the certificate holder and can be used to ensure the authenticity of digital signatures and messages, providing a level of non-repudiation.

71) Out of the listed options, the user account that contradicts the principle of non-repudiation is:

B. Shared account

Here's why a shared account is the most incongruent with non-repudiation:

Non-Repudiation: This principle ensures that someone cannot deny performing an action in a digital system.

Shared Accounts: By their very nature, shared accounts lack clear ownership of actions performed using the account. It becomes difficult to determine exactly who was responsible for a specific action taken under a shared account.

Imagine a scenario where a critical file is modified using a shared account. Determining who made the change becomes challenging, violating the principle of non-repudiation.

Let's explore why the other options are less relevant:

A. Standard user account: A standard user account can be traced back to a specific user, upholding non-repudiation.

C. Guest user account: Guest accounts typically have limited privileges and are used for temporary access. While they might not be ideal in all situations, they can still be linked to a specific machine or user.

D. Service account: Service accounts are used by system processes or applications to run specific tasks. They are often tied to a particular service and can be tracked for auditing purposes, maintaining non-repudiation.

72) Within the AAA security architecture, the aspect that handles confirming the identity of an individual or process is:

A. Authentication

Here's why authentication is the key component for identity verification:

Core Function: Authentication is the initial step in the AAA process. It verifies the claimed identity of a user or device attempting to access a network or system resource.

Verification Methods: Various methods can be used for authentication, including usernames and passwords, multi-factor authentication (MFA), digital certificates, or biometrics.

By successfully passing through authentication, a user or process is deemed legitimate and can proceed to the authorization stage.

Let's briefly explore the other parts of AAA for clarity:

Authorization: This stage determines what permissions or access rights are granted to a verified user or process. Even after successful authentication, a user might not have permission to perform certain actions or access specific resources.

Accounting: This final stage tracks and audits the activities of users and processes within a system. It records information about logins, resource usage, and other relevant actions.

73) You are absolutely right! In the AAA security architecture, the process of allowing or denying access to resources is called:

B. Authorization

Here's a breakdown of the AAA components:

Authentication: This verifies the identity of a user or device trying to access a system or network resource. Common methods include usernames and passwords, multi-factor authentication (MFA), digital certificates, or biometrics.

Authorization: Once a user or device is authenticated, authorization determines what permissions or access rights they have. Even with successful authentication, a user might not be authorized to perform certain actions or access specific resources based on predefined security policies.

Accounting: This final stage tracks and audits the activities of users and processes within a system. It records information about logins, resource usage, and other relevant actions.

So, authorization acts as the gatekeeper, deciding whether a verified user or device can access specific resources based on their assigned permissions.

74) In the AAA security architecture, the process of monitoring accessed services and the quantity of resources used is referred to as:

C. Accounting

Here's a breakdown of the AAA components:

Authentication: This verifies the identity of a user or device trying to access a system or network resource.

Authorization: Once a user or device is authenticated, authorization determines what permissions or access rights they have.

Accounting: This final stage tracks and audits the activities of users and processes within a system. It records information about logins, resource usage (such as storage space, network bandwidth, or CPU cycles), and other relevant actions. This information can be used for various purposes, including:

Identifying security risks or suspicious activity.

Optimizing resource allocation.

Generating billing reports (for metered services)

Demonstrating compliance with regulations.

75) Out of the listed options, several solutions offer AAA functionality:

B. TACACS+ (Terminal Access Controller Access Control System Plus): This is a widely used protocol for network access control that provides all three AAA functions (Authentication, Authorization, and Accounting).

D. RADIUS (Remote Authentication Dial-In User Service):

Another popular AAA protocol, RADIUS is commonly used for authenticating dial-up, VPN, and wireless network connections. It offers all AAA functionalities.

Let's explore why some options are not included:

A. CHAP (Challenge-Handshake Authentication Protocol): CHAP is an authentication protocol itself, but it doesn't handle authorization or accounting. It's often used in conjunction with other protocols like RADIUS for a complete AAA solution.

C. PAP (Password Authentication Protocol): Similar to CHAP, PAP is a basic authentication protocol and doesn't encompass authorization or accounting functionalities.

E. MS-CHAP (Microsoft Challenge Handshake Authentication Protocol): This is a proprietary Microsoft protocol that offers mutual authentication (verifying both server and client). While it focuses on authentication, it doesn't provide full AAA functionality.

76) Out of the listed options, three typical methods for authenticating individuals within the AAA framework include:

B. Usernames and passwords: This is the most common method for user authentication. Users identify themselves with a unique username and a corresponding password.

D. Biometrics: Biometric authentication relies on unique biological characteristics like fingerprints, facial recognition, iris scans, or voice recognition to verify a user's identity.

E. MFA (Multi-Factor Authentication): MFA adds an extra layer of security by requiring multiple authentication factors beyond just a username and password. This could involve factors like a one-time code sent via SMS, a security token, or fingerprint verification.

Let's break down why the other options are not typical authentication methods in AAA:

A. IP addresses: While IP addresses can be used for device identification, they are not reliable for user authentication. A single IP address can be shared by multiple users, and users can change IP addresses frequently.

C. MAC addresses: Similar to IP addresses, MAC addresses are unique identifiers for network devices but are not suitable for user authentication. They can be spoofed (faked) and don't necessarily identify individual users.

77) The common methods of device authentication in the AAA framework are:

B. Digital certificates: These are electronic documents used to verify the identity of a device, similar to how they're used for individuals.

C. IP addresses: These can be used to identify and authenticate devices on a network, although they can be spoofed or reassigned.

F. MAC addresses: These are unique identifiers assigned to network interfaces, commonly used for device authentication in local networks.

A, D, E. Usernames and passwords, MFA (Multi-Factor Authentication), and biometric authentication are typically used for authenticating individuals, not devices.

78) Out of the listed options, the BEST way to educate employees on recognizing phishing attempts is:

C. Conducting tailored phishing exercises with immediate

feedback for employees who fall for the simulated attack.

Here's why this option is most effective:

Hands-on Learning: Simulated phishing exercises provide a realistic experience that allows employees to test their knowledge and identify vulnerabilities in their ability to spot phishing attempts.

Targeted Training: Tailored exercises can be designed to address specific threats or scenarios relevant to the company and its employees. This makes the learning more relatable and impactful.

Immediate Feedback: Providing immediate feedback after the simulation is crucial. Employees can learn from their mistakes and understand the red flags associated with phishing emails.

Let's explore why the other options might not be as effective:

A. Quarterly Security Seminars: While informative, quarterly seminars might be too infrequent and cover a broad range of topics, potentially diluting the focus on phishing awareness.

B. Company-wide Email: A one-time email might not be enough to retain information in the long term, and employees might get overwhelmed or miss crucial details.

D. Monthly Newsletter: Similar to the email option, a monthly newsletter with a brief section might not provide enough depth or engagement to effectively educate employees.

Combining email tips with simulated exercises can be a powerful approach. The email can introduce general guidelines, and the exercises can provide practical application and feedback.

79) The statement is: "In a Zero Trust security model, resources

are accessible to everyone by default and Access is restricted based on user behavior or other analytics in a Zero Trust security model."

B. False

Zero Trust operates on the principle of "never trust, always verify". This means that access to resources is not granted by default, regardless of whether someone is inside or outside the network perimeter.

Here's a breakdown of the core principle in Zero Trust:

Least privilege access: Users and devices are granted only the minimum level of access required to perform their tasks. This reduces the potential damage if a breach occurs.

Continuous verification: User identities and device trust are continuously validated throughout a session, not just at login.

Micro-segmentation: The network is divided into smaller segments, limiting lateral movement within the network if a security breach occurs.

So, Zero Trust focuses on strict access control and verification, not on granting open access by default.

In a Zero Trust security model, the principle of 'never trusts, always verify' is upheld. This means that trust is not granted by default, even to individuals inside the network perimeter, and everyone attempting to access network resources must be verified. Therefore, the statement is false, as resources are not accessible to everyone by default.

80) Out of the listed options, the primary characteristic to consider when securing an environment that utilizes a real-time

operating system (RTOS) is:

B. Predictable timing and performance

Here's why predictability is crucial for RTOS security:

Real-Time Requirements: RTOS systems are often used in applications where timely responses are mission-critical. This could include industrial control systems, medical devices, or autonomous vehicles. Security measures cannot introduce unpredictable delays that could compromise the system's functionality.

Let's explore why the other options are not primary considerations for RTOS security:

A. Wide range of application compatibility: While compatibility is important, security focuses on protecting the system itself, not necessarily on supporting every possible application.

C. Focus on user interface design: RTOSes typically have minimal or no user interfaces. Security measures target system vulnerabilities, not user experience elements.

D. Multi-user support: Many RTOSes are designed for single-user environments or have limited multi-user functionality. Security considerations prioritize protecting the system from unauthorized access, regardless of the number of users.

A real-time operating system (RTOS) is engineered to handle data immediately upon arrival, often within a rigid time frame. This is critical for time-sensitive applications like those found in medical devices, industrial control systems, or automotive controls. Recognizing this characteristic is essential, as it shapes the implementation of security measures to avoid disrupting real-time processing needs.

81) Out of the listed options, the most likely direct impact of a company not complying with data protection regulations and the news becoming public is:

A. Reputational damage

Here's why reputational damage is the most likely consequence:

Public Perception: Data breaches and privacy violations can significantly erode public trust in a company. Customers might be hesitant to do business with an entity that mishandles their data.

Negative Press: News of non-compliance can lead to negative media coverage, further damaging the company's reputation. Social media can amplify the negative impact.

Let's explore why the other options are less likely direct consequences:

B. Service-Level Agreement renegotiation: While a data breach might lead to renegotiating service level agreements (SLAs) with partners or clients, this wouldn't be a direct consequence for the company itself. It would be a consequence of the reputational damage.

C. Annualized Loss Expectancy (ALE): ALE is a metric used to estimate the average annualized loss from security incidents. While non-compliance might increase the ALE, it's not a direct consequence but a potential financial risk.

D. Data ownership transfer: Data ownership transfer wouldn't be a typical direct consequence. Regulations might mandate stricter data protection measures or impose fines, but they wouldn't directly transfer ownership of the data.

Reputational damage occurs when an organization's reputation or esteem with clients, partners, and the public is harmed due to failures in meeting compliance obligations. Public disclosure of issues such as non-compliance with data protection regulations can greatly impact how the organization is viewed, potentially resulting in reduced trust and loss of business.

82) Out of the listed options, the most critical action to take after a network firewall upgrade is:

D. Update the security policies and network configuration documentation to reflect changes made by the new firewall.

Here's why updating documentation is crucial:

Maintaining Operational Efficiency: Accurate documentation ensures the security team and network administrators understand the new firewall's functionalities, configuration settings, and implemented security policies. This facilitates troubleshooting, managing future changes, and maintaining overall network security.

Reduced Risk: Outdated documentation can lead to confusion and misconfiguration, potentially introducing security vulnerabilities or operational inefficiencies.

Let's analyze the other options:

A. Penetration Testing: While penetration testing can be valuable to identify new vulnerabilities, it's not necessarily the most critical immediate action after an upgrade. Updating documentation is essential for ongoing network management. Penetration testing can be scheduled later as part of a comprehensive security assessment strategy.

B. Stakeholder Meeting: Discussing future upgrades might be a good long-term strategy, but it's not the most pressing task after the current upgrade. The immediate focus should be on understanding and documenting the implemented changes.

C. Implementing Additional Rules: While increasing security is desirable, adding firewall rules without proper review and documentation can lead to unintended consequences, potentially blocking legitimate traffic or creating unnecessary complexity. It's safer to document the existing configuration first before making further changes.

Documentation should always be kept up-to-date whenever modifications are made to the security infrastructure, including significant upgrades like installing a new firewall. This ensures that precise information is accessible for operating and maintaining the security controls, as well as for audit trails. Neglecting to update documentation can result in confusion, incorrect configuration, and security vulnerabilities. While the other options may be relevant in different scenarios, they do not directly tackle the essential requirement of maintaining accurate historical records of system configurations and policy modifications affecting security operations.

83) Out of the listed options, the authorization model that utilizes specific protocols to transfer user credentials across domains is:

D. Federated identity management

Here's why federated identity management stands out:

Cross-Domain Access: Federated identity allows users to authenticate with a single identity provider (IdP) and access resources in multiple security domains that trust the IdP. This eliminates the need for separate login credentials for each domain.

Underlying Protocols: Protocols like SAML (Security Assertion Markup Language), OAuth (Open Authorization), or OpenID Connect are used to exchange user authentication and authorization information between the IdP and the service providers (SPs) in the federated network.

Let's explore why the other options are not focused on cross-domain authorization transfer:

A. Mandatory Access Control (MAC): MAC enforces pre-defined access control rules based on security labels assigned to users, data, and resources. It doesn't involve separate domains or credential transfer.

B. Role-Based Access Control (RBAC): RBAC grants access based on a user's assigned roles within a system. It doesn't require interaction with external domains or protocols.

C. Discretionary Access Control (DAC): DAC allows the owner of a resource to control who can access it. It doesn't involve user authentication across domains.

Federated identity management specifically addresses the need for secure and centralized access control across multiple security domains.

Federated identity management enables a user's authenticated identity from one security domain to be recognized in other domains. This often involves using protocols like SAML and OpenID to enable Single Sign-On (SSO) functionality across various organizations or services. Discretionary Access Control (DAC) allows the resource owner to determine access permissions. Mandatory Access Control (MAC) grants access based on information clearance and classifications, and does not involve passing user information across security domains. Role-Based Access Control (RBAC) assigns permissions to roles rather than individual users, and is not specifically designed for sharing authentication and authorization data across different domains.

84) Correct answer: A. IaaS

Explanation:

Infrastructure as a Service (IaaS) allows the company to rent the infrastructure services such as servers, networking, storage, and virtualization from a service provider. This model would enable the company to avoid the costs and complexities of maintaining physical data centers while retaining control over their software applications running on the cloud infrastructure.

Infrastructure as a Service (IaaS) is a cloud model where a company rents infrastructure services (such as servers, networking, storage, and virtualization) from a service provider while retaining control over the software running on those resources. In Software as a Service (SaaS), the service provider offers a complete software solution for the company to use, such as Google Docs. Platform as a Service (PaaS) involves the service provider delivering a platform for development. Everything as a Service (XaaS) is a comprehensive term encompassing all service offerings.

85) Out of the listed options, the scenario-based discussion of disaster recovery plans and individual responsibilities is an example of:

B. Tabletop exercises

Here's why tabletop exercises are the most fitting choice:

Discussion and Planning: Tabletop exercises involve a group discussion around a simulated disaster scenario. Participants discuss potential problems, response strategies, and individual roles and responsibilities.

Low-Cost and Low-Risk: They require minimal resources and can be conducted without impacting production systems.

Let's analyze the other options:

A. Simulation: Simulations involve replicating a disaster scenario in a test environment using real systems or data. This is a more complex and resource-intensive approach compared to tabletop exercises.

C. Parallel processing: This refers to running multiple tasks simultaneously to improve efficiency. It's not directly related to disaster recovery testing.

D. Failover: Failover is the process of switching to a backup system in case of a primary system failure. It's an actual event that might occur during disaster recovery, not a testing method.

A tabletop exercise is similar to a simulation, but in a tabletop exercise, plans are only discussed, whereas a simulation involves a more hands-on walk-through of the steps.

86) Out of the listed control types, the most suitable option for analyzing a recent security incident is:

B. Detective controls

Here's why detective controls are ideal for post-incident

analysis:

Identifying the Attack: Detective controls help identify that an incident has already occurred. They analyze logs, system activity, and security alerts to detect suspicious activity or potential breaches. By analyzing the data collected by detective controls, you can understand how the attack unfolded and what vulnerabilities were exploited.

Let's explore why the other options are not as well-suited for this scenario:

A. Preventive controls: These controls aim to prevent security incidents from happening in the first place. While reviewing preventive controls might be part of the overall security assessment after an incident, the primary focus here is on understanding what happened, not necessarily what could have prevented it entirely.

C. Compensating controls: These controls provide temporary solutions to mitigate risks while a more permanent security fix is being developed. They wouldn't be the first choice for initial incident analysis.

D. Corrective controls: Corrective controls aim to fix the vulnerabilities that were exploited in the attack to prevent similar incidents in the future. However, this stage often comes after the analysis provided by detective controls helps identify the root cause of the problem.

Detective controls are intended to identify and respond to incidents that have occurred, enabling an organization to understand how the attack happened. By analyzing the incident, the organization can implement measures to prevent similar future attacks. Preventive controls aim to stop incidents before they occur, making them unsuitable for post-attack analysis.

Corrective controls are designed to limit damage after an incident and may not provide insight into the attack method. Compensating controls offer alternative security measures but do not focus on incident analysis.

87) Correct answer: B. Impossible travel

Explanation:

'Impossible travel' is the best indicator of potential unauthorized access in this context. It refers to the detection of logins from geographically distant locations within a short time frame that would be impossible for a legitimate user to achieve. This often signals credential compromise and unauthorized access. While 'Resource consumption' and 'Concurrent session usage' could suggest an issue, they do not specifically indicate unauthorized access as clearly as 'Impossible travel' does.

The correct answer is 'Impossible travel.' This indicator reveals unrealistic geographical locations between two login events by the same user within a short time frame, often indicating credential compromise and unauthorized access. While 'Resource consumption' and 'Concurrent session usage' might suggest an issue, they don't specifically indicate unauthorized access as clearly as impossible travel does.

88) Out of the listed options, the most suitable drive to fulfill the data encryption requirement for company laptops is:

D. SED (Self-Encrypting Drive)

Here's why SED is the best choice for on-device data encryption:

Hardware-Based Encryption: SEDs have built-in encryption

capabilities that automatically encrypt all data written to the drive. This encryption happens at the hardware level, transparent to the operating system and user, providing strong security.

Data Protection: Even if the laptop is lost or stolen, the data on the drive remains encrypted and inaccessible without the proper decryption key.

Let's explore why the other options are not ideal solutions:

A. PKI-SSD (Public Key Infrastructure Solid State Drive): While PKI can be used for encryption, it's not typically implemented directly on storage devices. PKI is more commonly used for digital certificates and secure communication.

B. VPN (Virtual Private Network): VPNs encrypt data in transit between the laptop and a remote network. They wouldn't directly encrypt data stored on the laptop's drive.

C. RAID 0 (Redundant Array of Independent Disks 0): RAID 0 is a striping technique that improves performance but doesn't offer any encryption functionality.

A Self-Encrypting Drive (SED) is a type of hard drive that automatically encrypts all data saved to the disk. It utilizes hardware-based encryption, meaning a circuit built into the disk drive controller manages the encryption and decryption processes. The entire contents of the drive, including the operating system and any user files or documents, are encrypted.

89) The correct answer is E. Honeytoken.

Explanation:

Honeypot refers to an entire fake system designed to attract and analyze attackers, rather than specific files or credentials.

DNS Sinkhole is used to redirect malicious traffic away from intended targets, not to create decoy data or credentials.

Honeynet is a network of honeypots, thus referring to a larger setup of fake systems.

Intrusion Detection System (IDS) is a security measure for monitoring network traffic and identifying suspicious activities, not for setting up decoy resources.

Honeytoken specifically refers to fake data or credentials planted to detect unauthorized access or data breaches, matching the description provided.

Firewall is a security measure to block or allow network traffic based on predetermined security rules, not a deceptive resource.

Therefore, the best description for the decoy files closely monitored for interactions is a Honeytoken.

Honeytokens are decoy credentials or data used to detect data breaches or unauthorized access within a network. Unlike honeypots, which are fake systems, honeytokens refer specifically to data or credentials. The correct answer is Honeytoken because it matches the description of a monitored fake resource containing seemingly valuable data. Other options, like Honeypot or Honeynet, typically refer to fake systems or larger network decoys, respectively, rather than specific pieces of data or credentials. IDS and Firewalls are security measures, not deceptive resources, and a Sinkhole is used for redirecting DNS traffic, not for data.

90) The most appropriate agreement to sign before sharing confidential information with a vendor about a new CRM

system is:

B. Non-Disclosure Agreement (NDA)

Here's why an NDA is the best choice:

Protecting Confidential Information: An NDA is a legal contract that protects confidential information disclosed between parties. It outlines what information is considered confidential and restricts the vendor from sharing it with unauthorized third parties without your consent.

Focus on Information Sharing: An NDA specifically addresses the protection of sensitive information during pre-contractual discussions. It's ideal for safeguarding your system specifications and data flow details before finalizing the partnership agreement.

Let's explore why the other options are not as suitable in this scenario:

A. Memorandum of Understanding (MOU): An MOU outlines the general terms of an agreement but is not legally binding in the same way as an NDA. It wouldn't provide the same level of protection for your confidential information.

C. Master Service Agreement (MSA): An MSA is a broader agreement that governs the overall terms and conditions of a service relationship. While it might include confidentiality clauses, it's typically signed after the project scope and deliverables are finalized, not before initial information sharing.

D. Service-Level Agreement (SLA): An SLA focuses on the specific metrics used to measure the performance of a service. It wouldn't be the primary agreement to address confidentiality concerns during initial discussions.

A Non-Disclosure Agreement (NDA) should be signed by the vendor before sharing any sensitive information. An NDA is a legal contract that creates a confidential relationship between the parties, ensuring that the shared information is used solely for the purposes specified in the agreement. NDAs are crucial for safeguarding sensitive information from unauthorized disclosure or misuse.

Feel free to reach out to me anytime, and don't forget to connect with me on LinkedIn: <u>Georgio Daccache</u>. I'm always available to provide additional assistance and support.

Good Luck

www.ingramcontent.com/pod-product-compliance
Lightning Source LLC
LaVergne TN
LVHW051439050326
832903LV00030BD/3171